IN IRELAND LONG AGO

In Ireland Long Ago

KEVIN DANAHER

THE MERCIER PRESS

DUBLIN and CORK

First published 1962
Reprinted 1964, 1967, 1969, 1976, 1978, 1986
© Kevin Danaher

ISBN 0 85342 781 X

Contents

Note: The Series of articles brought together in this book first appeared in *Biatas*, published by Comhlucht Siúicre Eireann Teoranta, between 1959 and 1962; they are republished here with the approval of the editors of *Biatas*

By Way of Introduction

The road ran past our gate, barely thirty yards from the front door. To the south it climbed over the hill where lay the bogs from which our turf came, to the small town and the railway station seven miles away. To the north it led to our own village, half a mile away, and there met other roads leading to all sorts of wonderful places, northwards to the Shannon, eastwards to the city and the plain of the Golden Vale, westwards to the great ocean. In winter it was deep in mud but in summer its dust was kind to little bare feet. Summer and winter we travelled it on foot or on bicycles to school and to Mass and on holiday expeditions that led farther and farther away as legs grew longer and stronger. Many the warm summer day we helped cottiers' children to herd a cow grazing the 'long meadow' – the grassy margin of the road – and felt the slow steady pulse of the countryside as it passed by. Older people walking, younger ones sailing past on bicycles, rails piled high with turf, carts full of clanking milk tankards, small herds of cattle on the way to a fair, children sent to the village for 'messages', occasionally a horseman or a tinker's spring cart or a motor-car that raised clouds of dust. When we were not yet as tall as a service rifle we had seen flying columns of the Republican Army marching past and wished we were a lot older. Twice or three times we hid in the dikes from a lorry load of Black and Tans – one of whose favourite recreations was the taking of pot-shots at 'moving targets', human or animal; poor men – they were monsters to us then, and only later did we realize that they were for the most part crazed with looted drink and with the fear of the swift vengeance that might at any moment speak a last word to them.

The road was our link with the world outside. Many of our people had travelled far on it, some never to return, some to come back to the quiet places. There was the man who stuck his spade in the potato ridge and climbed over the ditch to give directions to a bewildered foreigner in the fluent German he had learned in his twenty years in Milwaukee, and there were the two brothers who used to hold their private conversations in Maori. There was a man who had carried his pack over White Horse Pass on the trail to Klondyke and another who had marched through the Khyber Pass to Kabul and a very old man who had seen the approach of the relieving columns from his post on a roof in Lucknow. Another had laid telephone cables in Montevideo, another had dug gold in Kalgoorlie and another had punched cattle in Texas. The road linked us to many a distant corner of the world.

It was built in 1840 by men who were glad to get work at fourpence a day, some of them shoeless, some of them walking six miles to work in the morning's dark; the grandmother of our next door neighbour down the road missed a cake of soda bread from the window sill one day, to find that it had been taken by a poor boy who had had no food before coming to work. 'Only for the mercy of God it might have been one of my own' she said 'and take care would you pass the door again and you hungry, without coming in and eating whatever I have to give you'. It carried the wedding party and the funeral. It saw the Wran boys and the cross-roads dance. It bore the whole stream of a community's life. No wonder then, when I was asked to write for *Biatas* about country ways for country people, that my mind went back to the road and to the people who moved on it. Many of their ways begin to look strange to us now, more characteristic of the Middle Ages than of the modern world. They had their faults, God knows, but they were the faults of generosity. Some of them talked too much, a few drank too much, many were lacking in thrift, some had less than their due share of common sense. But they despised meanness and cruelty and treachery, and they never failed to give generously of what they had to those who had less than they.

The road is covered with shining tar macadam now, and cars, trucks and tractors roar along it. It is strung with telephone wires and electric cables and it is torn up at frequent although irregular intervals for the laying of water pipes. The pulse of life flows so much faster and the old ways are dying. And we who have seen both worlds may be allowed to recall the memories of the old ways and hope that the old virtues may survive.

Thatch and Whitewash

One of the most familiar sights of the Irish countryside is the old-fashioned farmhouse with its gleaming white walls and its roof of golden or grey-brown straw. So familiar, indeed, that to many it is an indispensable feature of the landscape, and no picture of Ireland is complete without it. And yet it is disappearing rapidly. Already it has gone from wide stretches of the land – you can travel the whole fifty-seven miles from Cork to Bantry without ever getting a glimpse of a thatched roof, and it may well be that the children of the present day will see the last survivors put away in a museum so that the future will not entirely forget what the past has been like. And they deserve a memorial, because they were good houses in their day, and sheltered many a generation of brave men and fine women.

At first sight they look very much the same all over Ireland. They are long, low buildings, one storey high, of a rectangular plan. They have strong thick walls which support a strong thick roof. They are made up of a number of rooms which open each into the next, for there is no central hallway or passage; and, usually, each room occupies the full width of the house – and as each room usually has one window in the front wall of the house, a count of the windows will give you the number of rooms. Commonest of all were the farmhouses with three apartments, a kitchen in the middle and a bedroom at each end, but the slightly smaller with two

apartments and the slightly larger with four were also
common. Still larger specimens, with five or six rooms,
may still be seen, but the smallest of all, the little one-
roomed house of the labourer, is almost quite vanished
now, replaced by successive schemes for the building of
'labourers' cottages' and county council houses. In passing we may note that the first of these schemes – in the
1880's – brought a new word into the Irish countryman's
vocabulary, the word 'cottage'. In England you may
speak of thatched cottages, but in Ireland every thatched
house is a 'house', and the word 'cottage' is confined to
the new slate-roofed dwellings built for the rural workers.

But to return to the old-fashioned farmhouses, the
general similarity in size and shape all over Ireland gives
a first impression that they are all alike. But a closer inspection shows many variations within the general
pattern. And many of the variations are of a local
character, so that a person who is accustomed to travelling about the country with open eyes will gradually
learn to place a particular specimen in its own district
with a fair degree of accuracy, and will never mistake a
photograph of a Wexford house for a Mayo one. There
are many reasons for this variation, not only the local
building methods and traditions and the local farming
economy, but also differences of soil and climate and
available materials. The last mentioned was very important, for the types of transport in use in the past did
not permit the ordinary man to bring his building
materials from afar. Nowadays we think nothing of
ordering a load of cement from a factory a hundred and
fifty miles away, or buying flooring and roofing timber
that may have grown in Canada or Finland, but a

couple of centuries ago only the very wealthy could have
heavy loads brought over long distances, and the
ordinary farmer had to use local materials for the walls
and the roof of his house. And so he built his walls of stone
and lime mortar, or stone and clay mortar, and over
wide areas the usual building material for the walls of
dwelling houses was tempered clay. And such a lot of
silly nonsense has been written by shortsighted tourists
and travellers in the nineteenth century about 'poor
mud cabins' that we must remind ourselves that tempered clay made and put up by expert hands was a very
good building stuff, and that most of the fine old thatched
houses which we see today are built of this material. A
few parts of the country built houses with 'dry walls',
that is to say of stone laid without mortar of any kind,
and built them so well that neither wind or rain penetrated. And a few mountain and moorland districts built
passable houses of blocks of turf cut from the bog.

The thatched roof deserves our attention, for it shows
many local varieties. The roof sheltered the whole house
and so bore the brunt of the local climatic conditions.
'Ní h-é lá na gaoithe lá na scolb' says the Irish proverb,
'The windy day is not the day for the scollops', a maxim
of warning to thatchers to choose the right kind of
weather for their work. With equal truth we might say
that the windy place is not the place for the scollops
either, for the type of roof known over most of the
country, with each course of straw held neatly down
by rows of scollops or withies would stand little chance
along the west coast against the Atlantic gales, and so
we find all the way down from Rathlin Island to Cape
Clear a type of roof in which the thatch is held on by a

stout network of ropes stretched firmly over the roof and secured to pegs in the wall tops or anchored with a row of stones. In the most exposed parts of north west Mayo and Donegal the thatched roofs are low and rounded at the top, for your typical roof of the midlands and the south east, with its sharp ridge and its row of ornamental straw 'bobbins' or 'dollies' would not last through the winter storm which pours smoothly and harmlessly over the roof evolved by local experience.

The general shape of the roof varies. All through the north and down the west you find high gables, while the south and east, for the most part, favoured the hip-roof which has thatch on the sloping ends as well as on the sides. And local opinion varies on the question of material, too. Most parts of the country seem to have preferred wheat straw, but Meath and Westmeath, Louth, Kildare, Offaly and Leix appear to favour oats straw, which, incidentally, has a beautiful golden colour when new. Some thatchers of the old school turned up their noses at anything but rye straw, and some would use only rye cut before the grain ripened. In all the six counties of Munster, the strong reed which grows wild in lakes and rivers is especially prized for first class thatching, while Derry, Donegal, Fermanagh and other parts of the north thought highly of flax thatch. Barley straw was very rarely used, but some mountain districts had strong, although rough-looking roofs of heather thatch. And there were areas which lacked straw and used rushes, *fineán*, bent-grass or other strong tough growths instead. Good straw for thatching is hard to get nowadays, for the straw which has been through the threshing machine or combine harvester is too crushed and broken to make a good roof. Expert thatchers, too, are becoming rare, and the cost of putting on a new coat of thatch has increased very greatly since the war. In different parts of the country, and with different material and methods, the life of a thatched roof varied. Some districts had to thatch every two or three years, and even the best reed thatch will not last more than twenty years, at the outside. Sooner or later, then, a new roof is needed. There is, too, the risk of fire in a thatched roof. All this adds up to spell the end of thatch as a roofing method, and certain it is that the building of a new thatched house will, in the future, be an event of such rarity that people will come from afar to see it done and its photograph will embellish the local newspaper.

A few districts of the eastern half of Ireland had, in the past, some two-storey thatched houses; an occasional survivor may still be seen. But this type was never common, and the one-storey house was the usual type all over the country. But most houses had lofts, either for storage or to increase the sleeping accommodation; the bed-loft was usually over the 'lower' room, and was lighted by a small window high in the gable or peeping under the thatched eave of the hip roof, and reached by a ladder or steep wooden stairs from the kitchen. On the night of a dance or a party in the kitchen these stairs gave seating accommodation to several sitting out couples, who had a grandstand view of the proceedings.

Windows and doors were usually made by the local tradesmen. Memories of the window-tax and of landlords and agents who were expert at smelling out signs of prosperity in order to have an excuse to raise the rent are still to be seen in some places in the fact that there are windows in the front of the house only, with none at all in the back. Another memory of former times is found in windows which cannot open at all, for it was strongly believed that fresh night air was harmful and should be excluded at all costs.

New ways of life and new fashions are calling for new houses. The thatched roof is doomed to extinction, together with many other features of the past. But there is one feature which we can, and should keep. In most parts of the country the walls were gleaming white, while a few areas went in for pale yellow, pink or blue. And this white or colour wash was one of the beauties of our landscape, while nothing is more drab and gloomy than the mean, utilitarian grey of raw concrete, which spread over the country like a rash in the nineteen-twenties, but which, happily, has fallen out of favour again as it deserved. Let us, then, hold on to the white-wash brush and be unsparing in its application at Christmas and Easter, and while we are about it, during the tourist season.

The Hearth

The hearth is the focal point of the old fashioned Irish
farmhouse. This is in keeping with a very ancient tradition; the very word *focus* meant a hearth in its original
Latin. In Ireland it always was found in the main room
of the house, the combined kitchen and living room. It
was towards the middle of the house and the wall behind
the fireplace separated the kitchen from the principal
bedroom. The hearth gave direction and orientation to
the whole house; the room – or rooms – beyond the
hearth wall were 'above' the kitchen, while a room off
the other end of the kitchen was always 'below'. If you
enquired for the man of the house and were told that he
was 'above in the room' or 'below in the room' you knew
at once where to turn to find him. Of course some larger
farmhouses had a parlour next 'above' the kitchen, but,
to tell the truth, this was seldom used except for the
important visitor who was ensconced there in state and
who, as often as not, would much prefer to join the
circle around the kitchen fire.

For the main hearth in the kitchen was not only the
centre of household work and activity but also the
centre of the social life of the house. Here the family sat
in the evening. Here the news of the day was discussed,
the stories were told and the ballads were sung. The
neighbour or friend who came in on an evening was bidden to come up to the fire and there was a shifting of
chairs to give him a good seat. Another friend dropped

in and the circle expanded again. If the old Grandad was a notable storyteller or the Granny knew all the old poems and ballads or Eileen had a fine voice for a song or Paddy played the fiddle or the squeezebox you could be sure of a wide circle around the friendly glow of the turf fire.

We are all heirs to this tradition. We turn instinctively towards the fireplace. On a warm summer evening you will find people in the towns sitting around an empty grate; even though it may be too warm to have a fire the hearth still draws them. In the ultra-modern flat which has some weird and wonderful method of heating and no fireplaces we feel somewhat lost, with nowhere to turn. In some European countries the table, not the hearth, is the social centre, and people sit at the table to chat and smoke. To an Irishman this looks like a conference or a committee meeting and as the evening goes on and there is no move to the fireside, and indeed no fireside to move to, he gets more and more restless. To us the table is a work place, whether with a chisel or a pen or a knife and fork, and when the job is done we move from the table, but the fireside is the place for rest and good talk and pleasant company.

There is always space for seats about the fire. The very large hearths of Munster and south Leinster have room for two chairs at each side of the fire, and the seats on the hearth are the seats of honour. In south Kerry and west Cork you'll see a large wooden seat, like a garden seat, on one side of the fire; four people can sit in comfort on it, or a tired man can lie full length on it, and many a wayfarer was thankful for a bed on it. Up the west, in Connaught and west Ulster, a couple of built-in stone seats, one at each side of the fire, may be found in almost every old farmhouse.

If you draw a line down the middle of one of the old style farmhouses, from end to end, that line will pass through the kitchen hearth. Across the northern part of the country, from Donegal to Antrim, there is a common type of small farmhouse with two rooms, the kitchen-livingroom and a bedroom, and in these houses the main fireplace is at one end of the house while there is another, smaller fireplace in the bedroom, at the other end. In these houses a chimney crowns each gable, but in most other parts of the country the chimney rises above the roof ridge somewhere towards the middle of the house. Most of the old chimneys are massive masonry affairs, but many a smaller house in the past, and not a few larger ones, had chimneys made of lath-and-plaster or wattle-and-clay and these, naturally, must have a lighter chimney stack, of brick or of wood, or just the upper end of the chimney funnel thatched around. There are still a few survivors of these types to be seen.

Of course none of these features is exclusively Irish. The fireplace on the central axis of the house is usual in much of western Europe, but a little farther east other varieties are found. In most Swedish farmhouses of the old style the fireplace is in a corner of the kitchen. In central Europe the fire is enclosed in a stove and the blaze can be seen only when the door of the stove is opened. In the old fashioned Russian farmhouses the stove or oven was a large low structure, so wide that the beds could be made on top of it during the bitter cold of winter. In warmer countries to the south there is no need of a fire for comfort, and the cooking hearth may be at a distance from the living quarters, sometimes even in another building.

Keeping the fire burning meant much work for the farmer and his workpeople. In most parts of Ireland the traditional fuel is turf. This meant long days in the bog harvesting the year's supply. Every sod of turf was handled many times, in cutting and spreading and footing, in drawing out and loading and unloading and ricking and clamping, and finally in keeping the fire built up to just the right degree needed for whatever was being done. In fine weather the work in the bog was pleasant enough, but if the early summer came bad it could be heartbreaking. In most houses the turf fire was kept alive under the ashes all night and revived again first thing in the morning. It might burn in this way for long years. Recently an old woman in County Limerick expressed her one regret on moving into a fine new house – the fire that had burned continuously on the old hearth for three hundred and thirty years was now gone out for ever.

Outside the turf areas fuel was not so easy to get. Of course there was imported coal, still called 'sea-coal' in some parts of Ireland, because it came across the sea, but wood must have provided most of the firing in the days when there still were great forests in the country. The lighter varieties of firewood, 'brosna' or 'faggot' or 'kippens', were always welcome, and the gathering of these was often the children's job. Parts of County Kilkenny and County Carlow have burned the local anthracite for centuries. It had to be ground small and mixed with clay and formed into balls – locally called 'boms' – before it could be burned on the hearth. And some kind of draught had to be provided. In later years the wheel-bellows was used, but in former times there were draught channels, called 'shores' or 'flukes' leading under the floor from the hearth to outside the house, one to each side, and by stopping the one on the sheltered side a draught was induced in the other. The wheel-bellows have spread outside this area, to cover all of south Leinster and east Munster; it is also used in parts of south-east Ulster, in Armagh and Down and parts of Louth, Cavan and Monaghan. In Carlow and Kilkenny some of the old anthracite mills may still be seen. A central upright pivot holds a shaft which passes through a great disc of stone, four or five feet high and a couple of feet thick. A patient horse tackled to the shaft walked round in a circle pulling the roller round and round while men with shovels threw the lumps of anthracite before it and scraped off the powder behind it. Animal dropping, especially cowdung, were dried and collected to supplement the fuel supply in some areas. This, too is an old and widespread tradition; the desert Arabs burn camel droppings and the Red Indians of the American prairie used those of the bison.

Only the very largest farmhouses had a boiler in the yard, so that for the most part all the water heating and boiling of food for animals, as well as the household cooking, were done on the kitchen hearth. Most farmhouse hearths boasted a crane, an upright iron pivot, four or five feet high, with a long projecting arm suitably braced to carry the pots and other utensils which were hung from it on a variety of hooks and hangers. Most cranes had a rack which could be adjusted for height, and many had elaborate levers whereby heavy pots could easily be raised and lowered as required. But the main advantage of the crane was that it allowed a large pot of boiling liquid to be swung clear of the fire and the contents tipped into a tub or bucket with safety to the operator. A fine crane was the pride of the blacksmith who made it and of the house that owned it.

In nearly every part of Ireland the kitchen fire was at floor level, not raised in a grate. Portions of the fire could be moved about the hearth, and often there were three or four different fires at work, the main one under the big pot, a smaller one baking a bastable of bread, the teapot sitting on a third and a fourth heating a flat-iron. As to cooking, most of the food was boiled, whether it was porridge or meat or potatoes or vegetables, although the bastable or pot-oven could bake a joint or a fowl to the taste of an epicure, and there was always the frying pan. Potatoes might be roasted in their jackets in the embers – the old people always said they tasted best like that. In some farmhouses meat was roasted on spits; you can still see the slots which held the spits in the old dressers. The spit was a slender iron bar, up to four feet long, bent into a crank at one end. It was stuck through the joint or fowl to be roasted and supported at each end by a little iron stand, so that the meat was close to the fire, while a pan underneath caught the dropping juice and fat. But few people now alive can remember the spit in use, and there is hardly a survivor who, in the old days, was entrusted with the task of turning the crank to expose all sides of the meat to the heat of the fire.

There are memories of still older cooking methods. Fowl or game birds were completely covered, feathers and all, in a couple of inches of yellow or blue clay and put into a hot fire. When sufficient time had elapsed the lump, now as hard as stone, was drawn out and broken open. Off came the crust of clay and with it the feathers and skin, and the meat inside was perfectly cooked without the loss of a single drop of juice. Strangest of all was a method employed by hunters and soldiers, when cooking in the open air. The skin of a newly killed animal was tied into the shape of a bag and this was filled with water and pieces of the meat and hung on stakes over a fire. The liquid inside kept the skin from burning, and so the water boiled and the meat was cooked.

Much of this is ancient history now. The old open hearth has had its day and is now becoming obsolete. The anthracite range, the electric cooker, the paraffin or container-gas stove have largely taken its place. The housewife's work is lightened, but another link with the past is broken.

The Light and the Fire

A man spends about a half of his life in the dark. In the summer he does not notice it, but in the long winter nights it is all too apparent. Of course, much of the period of darkness is devoted to sleep, but it is only natural that mankind, from the very earliest times, wished for some kind of light to relieve the oppression of the night and did his best to find it. We know that our remote ancestors made fires at the mouth of their caves as much for the cheerful light as for the heat which they gave, and crude stone 'lamps' have been found in some of the caves which our more recent forebears, of twenty thousand years or so ago, decorated with paintings which are still splendid pieces of art. Yet with all this desire for light, and all the urgent need of it, it is only recently that any advance has been made from the most primitive forms of illumination. The 'lamps' of the stone age men were just stones with little hollows in them; a drop of fat or blubber oil was put in the hollow with a bit of moss or string for a wick, and there was your lamp. People still alive have seen the same kind of lamp – a small dish or bowl of oil with a floating wick – in common use. We can see it still in ceremonial use in the sanctuary lamps of the churches.

It was only a hundred and fifty years or so ago that anyone thought of an enclosed wick and a glass chimney for the oil lamp, and it is only just over a hundred years ago that any oil other than the natural animal, fish or vegetable oil came into use. The paraffin lamp dates from the eighteen fifties. It is astonishing to think that all the progress of civilisation, all the philosophy of Greece, all the organisation of Rome, all the monks and scholars and scientists of all the centuries never made the slightest advance beyond the crudest of oil lamps and candles until the time of our own grandfathers. Nowadays it is only when the electric current fails during a storm, or when we have forgotten to order a new container of gas, that we realise what it is to live with poor illumination, and the very poorest we know, the paraffin candle or the storm lantern, are miles ahead of anything available to our great-grandfathers.

The little pan of oil with a wick sticking out of it was used mainly along the coast, for the fisher people had an easy source of oil from fish, seals and creatures of the whale family. In many places a large cockle or scallop shell formed the lamp; a little wooden frame was made to hold the shell and hang it on the wall. Others had a little iron dish, very like a sauce boat; the wick lay in the spout and a second little dish caught any drip. Still others preferred a small vessel like a teapot with a wick stuck in the spout. All of them were smoky and gave hardly as much light as a good candle, but, no doubt, the people of the time thought them a very big advance on the bogdeal splinter which was a well-known source of light and by which people worked and even read and wrote.

Candles were used by the ancient Romans, and the virtues of the beeswax candle are known since that time, but beeswax was an expensive commodity, for use only in church ceremonial or on festive occasions. The ordinary man had to do with tallow, that is, melted animal fat. Whenever an animal was killed the suitable parts of the fat were set aside for tallow. Tallow rush-lights were in common use; to make them rushes w re picked and peeled so that one narrow strip of skin heid the pith together and allowed to dry. The tallow was melted in a vessel called a 'grisset', a little boat-shaped dish with a handle like a frying pan and three legs to support it over the fire; the shape of the grisset made the drawing of the rushes through the fat easy. There were special holders for the rushlights, with jaws like forceps or tongs, often combined with a candlestick so that either candle or rushlight could be used as required. The next form of candle was the 'dip', which was made by dipping a wick into a vessel of melted tallow; this formed a coat around the wick, and any thickness could be reached by successive dips and coolings. A really skilful worker could make very smooth and even dips, but the average one was lumpy and uneven, which did not help the burning. Better again were the moulded candles made in the brass or pewter moulds which are still to be seen in old farmhouses. These moulds look just like the barrel of a bicycle pump but are pointed at the closed end which is pierced by a hole for the wick. They came in various sizes and thicknesses, so that a variety of candles could be made. The parish clerk had a special set of moulds for making the church candles, which, of course, had at least a proportion of beeswax. The bees-wax candles, among other advantages, smelled sweetly, but a tallow candle, especially a poorly made one of bad tallow, could make an unpleasant stink. Some people made candles of resin, melted and cast in a mould with a central wick, and these burned with a good flame and had a sharp but not displeasing smell.

If the Romans failed to develop artificial light they were very advanced in the matter of heating. A Roman of any degree of prosperity had central heating produced by the passage of smoke and hot air from a fire through pipes or channels under the floors. This was quite the normal thing. But the idea was lost in the downfall of Rome fifteen or sixteen hundred years ago, and is only coming back in our own time. Meanwhile our ancestors' idea of a good heating system hardly got beyond the open hearth, with a few refinements, such as wall ovens, bellows or slightly raised grates, and even our own fireplaces of today are very little more than open hearths with 'trimmings'.

Down through the ages, until quite recently, Ireland was a well wooded country. It is only since 1600 that the woods began to be cut away to such an extent that the country became bare of trees. We can be sure that very many parts of the country depended upon timber for their fuel in the old days, and that the fuel harvest during the summer and autumn consisted of the felling and chopping up of trees, the search in the forest for dead branches and the storing of big piles of logs and brushwood. We can be sure, too, that they knew a great deal about timber as a fuel, what kinds were best for a quick fire, or for different methods of cooking or to 'keep the fire in'. Any farmer would know the burning properties of the various woods, oak, pine, ash, elm and so on, and what sort of fire they would make. There were charcoal burners at work in the woods, too, making the charcoal needed by the blacksmith and other craftsman, and by the little iron smelting furnaces which were busily at work. But all that is lost now with much more woodland lore. Many a man of our day, an expert on turf, has very little acquaintance with wood as a fuel.

The early Irish laws, the 'Brehon Laws', make mention of bogs and of turf-cutting, but are concerned only with rights and compensation for trespass and other such legal matters. The humdrum matter of how the turf was harvested was, as we might expect, far below the notice of the learned lawyers of a thousand years ago. However, the mention does show that turf cutting was well-known then, and we can assume that it was a common practice even in still more ancient times. Probably not to the same extent as in recent times, for the forests gave firing to many people; it was a matter of local supply, especially as the possible carting distance was limited. Turf is still cut and saved in every county in Ireland and the method is much the same everywhere. Experts will argue the advantages of 'breast sleán' and 'foot sleán' or uphold the method of 'brainshing' with three-pronged forks against the more common method of spreading with the wheelbarrow, and the various types of bog and grades of turf are as an open book to your knowledgeable bogman. But the devotees of 'made turf' or, as others call it, 'puddled turf' will back their product against any other kind, and in all fairness we must be prepared to agree with them often, if not always. Turf is 'puddled' by digging out the turf mould, the 'bog stuff', mashing it up and forming it into sods with the hands. It is the same method which produces the modern turf briquettes, and gives results which burn just as well even if the sods are much rougher in appearance.

One part of Ireland looked down upon turf and had little need of big stacks of firewood. The area within carting reach of the anthracite pits of the Castlecomer district had its own form of fuel and a very high opinion of its value. Anthracite will not burn in an open hearth, but they knew the answer to that one. For one thing, the coal was crushed finely in special mills – of which many are still to be seen – and mixed with clay and water so that it could be formed into lumps, known as 'boms'. And for another, raised grates were found to give better results, so raised grates have been common in the area for a much longer time than in other parts of Ireland.

In the matter of both fuel and light we have come in one stride from the ancient way to the most modern. Our grandfathers and grandmothers in the countryside used the same methods as their ancestors of a thousand or two thousand years before, with the open hearth and the tallow candle. Now we may select from a large variety of lighting and heating methods and appliances that turn night into day and winter into summer, an advance which may be less spectacular than television or jet aircraft but is in fact much more important to us all.

Pots and Pans

In some parts of the country the outside of the old style farmhouse has changed very little over the years. New types of houses there are in plenty, but those who can still afford the luxury of a thatched roof keep to the old tradition as regards the exterior of the house. But step inside the kitchen, and what a change! Your grandmother wouldn't know the place, or have the least notion of what to do with all the electrical gadgets. Twenty years ago we were clamouring for electricity in the countryside; now we have it. Our present drive is for running water, with kitchen sink and bathroom in every farmhouse, and these will be in every farmhouse within a few years. Then good bye to drudgery and wasted effort, and, incidentally, good bye to a whole series of quaint and curious gadgets which formed the household equipment or our grandmothers fifty or sixty years ago.

This change is due, not to rural electrification and running water; indeed they have been brought by the change rather than been the cause of it. It is the new idea, the coming into our quiet countryside of the brave new world, with its heralds the newspaper, the magazine, the film, the radio and the television – the feeling of belonging to a new age and wishing to share in all it can give. Hence the shining machines, the bright chromium plating and stainless steel, the gay-coloured plastics.

But don't let us be misled by all this splendour into

thinking that great-granny spent her time crouched over a smokey hearth stirring a skillet. No, indeed. Her kitchen had its bright spots, too, with shining copper and 'chaneys' and lustre jugs which now are the delight of the antique dealer, most of them hand made by good craftsmen, and all the better for that. The coming of the mass-production factory and the chain store has meant the end of the local craftsmen's market, and the craftsmen's products are vanishing like snow in summer. Things made of wood or iron or leather have an amazingly short life once they are laid aside from daily use, they dry up or rust and fall to bits, especially when they are heaved into the back of the loft or the outhouse by an energetic young housewife who is determined to be up to the very latest fashion. She will probably live to see her daughters bewailing the loss of their background and reverently placing the sole survivor – grandmother's pewter jug, or greatgrand aunty Katey's willow pattern dish – in a place of honour. But the simple, humdrum, everyday things will have gone for good and all, and even their use, their very existence, will be forgotten.

Take, for instance, all the containers. Things to keep this and that in. There was the flour bin, with two compartments, one for flour and the other for meal – which might be wholemeal or 'yalla meal'. In some houses the grain for human consumption, or the meal, especially the oatmeal, was kept in large chests, when packing the meal in, the children used to stamp it down firm with their bare feet. Other chests held the clothing, the spare sheets and blankets, the woven cloth and linen kept for making garments as required, the chests set aside for the daughters' wedding clothes and linen. These clothes chests were made very well, with tight-fitting lids, to keep out the moth, and chests of all kinds did duty as seats when necessary. Many things were kept in bags which hung on the wall, especially woollen thread and sewing and knitting materials – the bags kept them clean from dust and smoke. We are told that in ancient times it was the monks' custom to keep their books in leather bags hung on the wall. A special box for needles – usually a small neat wooden box bought from a pedlar – was prized by many a housewife. The salt box hung near the hearth, to keep the salt dry, and the 'knife box' did not hold the knives – it was a board with a small box at the end; the box held a piece of bath brick with which the knives were cleaned on the board, for there were no 'stainless' blades then. Tea and sugar were usually kept in tin boxes, although the tea sometimes came in the boxes of lacquered wood in which it had been exported from Canton. One of these Chinese boxes turns up now and then, even yet, in an old farmhouse.

Then there were the baskets of all sorts. Some big and some small, some fitted with lids, some without. Potatoes were kept in large baskets, eggs in smaller ones. But baskets were more for carrying things than for keeping things in; the dinner to the men in the field, the eggs to the market and the children's books to school, as well as the turf, the fish, the seaweed carried in the big back-baskets. In some places baskets were used to hold food on the table, such as bread or potatoes, and often food was kept hot in a basket, a round flat basket of peeled rods, placed over the mouth of a large pot full of hot water, when the steam, rising through the basket, kept the dinner moist as well as warm. It was pleasant to sit round such a basket and eat directly from it on a cold day. Many kinds of baskets and bags were woven from straw or rushes, some very neatly and skilfully; there were bags of cloth and hide too.

Curiously enough, our ancestors went in very little for preserved food. 'The newest of food and the oldest of drink', as the proverb says. Meat and fish salted in barrels for a time and then hung from the rafters were the only preserved foods used extensively. A large barrel – one that had held some imported liquid, or one made locally by the cooper – was used for the salting, and it often made the rounds of the townland, used in one house after another, according as the pigs were killed. Some places went in for a bacon box hanging from the roof, but for the most part the flitches hung, glistening with salt, from the 'meat stick', a stout beam fitted with many hooks.

The containers for liquids were many. There were the crocks, bowls and pans for the milk. These were made by local potters who sent men about to the fairs and markets with a selection of their products. They made stoneware jugs and jars too; the jars were popular for taking milk or buttermilk to the workers in the fields – they were easy to cork and kept the liquid cool – and for keeping still more palatable drinks such as stout and whiskey. Then there were many kinds of wooden vessels, mostly made by the coopers or the turners. The coopers made their vessels of staves bound with hoops. Vessels and containers for liquids were made of oak, while those for dry substances (for instance, butter firkins) were made of beech, ash, sycamore or deal. Some first class work was done in bogdeal. The cooper's

main work was the making of casks and barrels of all
sizes from 'pipes' and 'puncheons' holding up to 120
gallons to little kegs of a gallon measure. Casks for beer
and porter, wine and oil and brandy, and casks for salt
meat, beans, biscuits and the other provisions needed on
board ship, as well as great casks to hold fresh water on
long voyages. Coopers were kept busy in the seaports on
this work. Cork was a famous town for ships' stores, as
well as for the great butter market, and the Cork coopers
were famous too; when Arthur Young was there in 1776,
he found 700 coopers at work. Many household utensils
were made by coopers. Churns, for instance, and several
kinds of milk cans, as well as firkins for butter, keelers –
wide tubs with low sides – used to set milk so that the
cream could be skimmed off, buckets, and several sizes
of drinking vessels. Some of these last were handsome
articles; some of them very small, holding a half pint or
so, with neat hoops of wood or metal. Some houses had
little kegs mounted on stands, with small wooden taps;
these held whiskey or wine, and could be placed on the
table when a guest came. Made of polished wood and
with brass or copper hoops these little containers made
a brave show. Some of the drinking vessels had handles
attached, others had one stave longer than the others
sticking up as a handle.

Another maker of wooden vessels was the turner, who
took a piece of timber, put it in his lathe and turned a
wooden cup or bowl from it. Plates, dishes, egg stands,
piggins and noggins were just as easy, and the pole lathe
used by the country turners had one great merit – the
motion of the work was reciprocal, that is, the piece of
wood being turned was spun first in one direction, and

then in the other, backwards and forwards, and not just all in one direction as in the modern types of lathe, so the turner could make a vessel with a projecting handle all in one piece. Beech was the favourite wood, and when the vessels were well washed they had a lovely satiny cream surface and were the pride of the housewife's dresser. There was still another type of wooden vessel, those carved by hand out of a chunk of wood, and these could be of any shape or size; some of them were fine and decorative, others botched and crude, according to the skill of the maker.

Strange as it may seem it was quite easy to heat and even to boil liquids in a wooden vessel. All you had to do was to heat some smallish round stones in the fire and drop them into the liquid – a quick dip of the stone in a vessel of water washed off the soot or ashes without any great loss of heat. You just kept on doing this until the milk, or whatever it was, boiled. But metal vessels were usual for cooking, even from a very early time, and boiling or stewing – a relatively advanced form of cooking, much more so than the primitive roasting over an open fire – was the usual method for most foods. The handsome bronze cauldrons displayed in the National Museum are anything up to two thousand years old; they are cooking vessels, and not for storage; they are round bottomed and will not stand steady without some form of support. They were hung over the fire, of course, and we are told that some of them were large enough to cook a yearling bullock and a pig at the same time.

Bronze vessels were valuable and comparatively rare, and it was not until about four hundred years ago when cast iron articles began to be produced in quantities, that one would expect to find several iron pots in an ordinary man's house. The familiar three legged pot, and the 'sauce pan' – the round pot with a long handle, come from that time and are still in use, and the same is true of the frying pan and the cast iron griddle. Copper pots and pans were highly thought of. They were very good cooking vessels and looked very handsome, but they cost a lot more than the plain iron ones, and not everybody could afford to have them. There were copper tea-kettles, jelly-moulds, salt shakers, pepper pots, strainers and colanders and hot water cans. There were many articles of pewter, drinking vessels, plates, soup tureens, jugs, cruet stands and teapots, and wealthy people had these made of silver.

A regular sight at fairs and markets was the 'chaney seller' with his (or her, for many were women) stock of jugs, bowls, dishes and cups. Up to sixty or seventy years ago the usual drinking vessel in the countryside was the china or stoneware bowl, holding about a pint and very comfortable to cold hands on a winter's day. They are still in use in parts of the Continent, and anyone who has enjoyed a bowl of coffee at a small French inn will testify how far superior they are to the cups brought in by the 'refinement' of late Victorian times. This explains the multitude of bowls still sometimes to be seen on a farmhouse dresser.

Sieves and strainers were there in plenty. Some were of metal, tinplate or copper, but most were of leather or wood. A sheepskin stretched on a hoop and pierced with holes of suitable size, or a hoop laced across with thin strips of wood, these were the favourite types, and the sieve maker had a whole range of sizes and kinds to sieve or strain almost anything. Tightly woven or without holes they made a useful carrying utensil. A rough specimen could be made by almost any handyman, and we can be sure that many such crude expedients were in use among the less houseproud. The travelling tinsmiths, our old friends the tinkers, were another useful source of supply of cheap metal utensils, for metal working of any kind was beyond the scope of the ordinary countryman.

So that our great-grandmothers were not badly provided with pots, pans and things about the kitchen.

What did they Eat?

What sort of food did our ancestors eat in times gone by? Sometimes we get the impression that Ireland, in ancient times, was a land of plenty, and again we get quite the opposite impression – that our forebears lived out their lives on the very edge of starvation. In reality both these impressions are wrong. There were good times when there was more than enough for all, and bad times when everybody was on short rations. But for the most part the position was as it has been in most parts of the world at most times; the well-to-do had an excess of good things to the point of luxury, the ordinary folk of the country-side had a rough plenty, but there were poor folk who were short of even the necessaries of life and there were destitute individuals who depended for their existence on the charity of their neighbours.

It is only during the last three hundred years that the potato became common in Ireland. Before its coming there were two main sources of food, namely corn and cattle. Corn meant bread and porridge, and cattle meant milk products and meat products. And it seems certain that at most times and in most parts of the country the raising of cattle was more important than the growing of crops. The number of cattle in the country was enormous and the herding of cattle was regarded as an occupation superior to that of digging in the soil. A man's wealth was reckoned by the number of his cattle; we still reckon the size of a farm as the 'grass of so many cows',

In ancient times much less hay was available than is now the case, and whatever winter fodder there was had to be saved for the milking and breeding cattle. So it was the custom to dispose of many of the bull calves while quite young, a custom which held on in parts of Ireland until quite recently. This meant fresh veal several times a year. It was also necessary to kill off some of the dry stock at the coming of winter, about November Day, and large portions of the meat were salted down for use during the winter. We know, too, that large herds of sheep and pigs were kept. The sheep, as now, were pastured in open country or on the hills, but the pigs were kept in big herds in the woods, especially in oak woods where they ate the acorns fallen from the trees. This gave a varied meat supply, of beef, veal, mutton and pork, as well as salted meats, especially salt beef and bacon. And we must not forget that game was then more plentiful in the great woods that covered much of the country. There were deer and hares and wild boar in plenty, as well as game birds. Some of these were salted, too. We hear of salt venison as a delicacy; indeed all salt meat was highly valued, possibly because salt was not so easy to get then as now, and usually salted meat was worth twice as much as an equal quantity of fresh meat.

The meat was roasted or boiled. In the house of a chieftain or other important man there was always a great cauldron to boil large quantities of meat for the household. And people sat around the fire gossiping and getting in the cook's way in those old times just as they sometimes do now. But they did so at their own risk. The Brehon Laws, which go into great detail about many everyday things, lay down very clearly that the cook is not responsible for splashing hot broth on those at the fire if he gives warning in a loud voice 'Look out! Here goes the fork into the cauldron!'

As to roasting, one ancient tale describes the cook, in clean linen cap and apron, cooking for the King of Munster. The cook calls for juicy old bacon and corned beef and fat mutton, and a comb full of honey and salt in a silver dish. Then he lights a fire of clean ash wood and sets up the portions of meat before it on white hazel spits, and as the meat cooks he runs about the fire rubbing salt and honey into one piece after the other.

Fish was eaten, too, in places close to the sea or to the rivers and lakes – and what part of Ireland is not? Salmon was then, as now, the most highly prized fish, and, like the meat, was eaten with a flavouring of honey. Often a dish of honey was put on the table, and each diner could use it as we use bottled sauces.

The carving of the meat was a matter of some ceremony. Certain people had to get certain portions, and many a quarrel arose because some arrogant warrior considered himself slighted by being given a slice a shade inferior to that given to his rival. The custom of giving the head of the killed beast to the blacksmith is a recent survival of this old practice.

The blood of the animals was saved and cooked – as it still is in black puddings. And there was the practice, in times of scarcity, of drawing some blood from the living beasts, both cattle and horses, and cooking it for food; this was done up to quite recently, almost within living memory. Marrow-bones are mentioned, too, as a delicacy.

Some types of meat mentioned in the old records are no longer eaten. One text advises that horseflesh should not be given to people recovering from illness, as it is too strong. We may conclude from this that healthy people did eat horseflesh, as people still do on the Continent. The meat of the badger is mentioned as a delicacy. Up to quite recently the fisher people along our west coast ate the meat of both seals and porpoises, and according to one author, preferred the meat of the 'sea-pig' (porpoise) to that of any land pig.

As to milk and milk products, they were highly valued and formed a very important part of the everyday diet. Butter was consumed in great quantities, not only fresh but also well salted. Sometimes it was flavoured with herbs and enclosed in a wooden vessel and buried in a bog to be preserved and matured. We still come on vessels of this bog-butter during turf cutting and other bog work. Curds and cheese were also eaten, and in some places cheese was made of sheep's milk.

Eggs were in common use. Goose eggs were looked upon as a delicacy, and the eggs of wild birds, especially sea-birds, were collected in great numbers.

Except for cereals – bread and porridge of wheat, oats, barley or rye – there was not much consumption of vegetable products. Cabbage was grown, and some types of root-crops of the carrot and parsnip kind, but apparently in small quantities. Some wild growths, such as nettles and *praiseach bhuí*, were boiled and eaten, but, on the whole, the vegetable products were used as flavouring or 'kitchen' rather than as the main food. Honey and salt appear to have been the main flavourings. Honey was of much more importance when there was no sugar known. Onions, leeks and garlic were all known and relished, as were watercress and sorrel. Apples were cultivated, and wild fruits such as sloes, raspberries and strawberries, crabapples and whortleberries, blackberries and hazelnuts were eaten in the summer and autumn when they were ripe.

Thus we have, from ancient times, a picture of a good and fairly varied diet. People who visited Ireland in later centuries often remarked on the fruitfulness of the land, and the excellence and abundance of the food. When the Papal Nuncio, Archbishop Rinuccini, came to Ireland in 1645, his secretary wrote back to Italy that the people were well-nourished 'Butter is used abundantly. There is plenty of fruit, apples, pears, plums and artichokes. All foodstuffs are cheap. A fat bullock costs sixteen shillings, a sheep one and three pence, a pair of fowls five pence, eggs four for a penny. A good sized fish costs a penny. We bought a thousand pilchards or oysters for a shilling'. A few years later, after Cromwell had wasted the country, there was scarcity, but a few years later still when the people had had time to recover, food again became plentiful and cheap. A Frenchman who was here in 1672 reported that butter and cheese cost a penny a pound. Beef, mutton or veal a penny a pound. A salmon for threepence, a codfish for twopence, a pair of large soles for a penny, a hundred herrings for threepence. 'In fact' he says, 'this is a land of plenty. If you drink only twopence worth of beer in a public house, they will give you as much bread, meat, butter, cheese and fish as you like, and you only pay your twopence for the beer.' Of course, you had to have the twopence, or you got none of these good things. The poorer people fared more simply. Sir William Petty, writing at the same time as our Frenchman, tells us 'Their food is bread in cakes, whereof a penny serves a week for each; potatoes from August till May, mussels, cockles and oysters near the sea, eggs, and butter made very rancid by keeping in bogs. As for flesh, they seldom eat it, unless it be of the smaller animals, because it is inconvenient for one of these families to kill a beef, which they have no convenience to save. So as 'tis easier for them to have a hen or a rabbit than a piece of beef of equal substance'.

This was written three hundred years ago, and already shows that the potato was becoming an important part of the people's food. The reluctance of people to kill a large animal, such as a bullock, because it would give them far too much fresh meat which could not be saved if salt were scarce is a normal feature of rural life in more recent times. Farmers killed, and still kill, smaller animals such as a pig, or in mountain districts, a sheep, but not a cow or a bullock. The smaller animal could be shared round among a circle of neighbours even if very little of it were salted down, and when each neighbour killed an animal in turn, fresh meat was had by all at fairly frequent intervals. Sir William Petty also mentions the shellfish gathered on the shore, which formed an important part of the diet of seaside dwellers. He might also have mentioned, as other writers do, the eating of *dilisc*, *sleamhchán* and *caraigín*, three edible seaweeds which are still used, though not as much as formerly.

The last hundred years has seen a very big change in our eating habits. Many of the old-fashioned foods have been discarded in favour of those now bought from the local shops. This change was brought about more by social than by economic considerations. It was more a fashion than a necessity. Certain kinds of food became associated with a more inferior social position or with a lower standard of life. That this association was quite wrong is shown by the fact that most of these foods are still very popular in other parts of north-western Europe, particularly in Norway and Sweden, where the standard of living is high. Nevertheless it became fixed in peoples' minds in Ireland that there was something to be ashamed of in the eating of porridge, oatcakes, salt herrings, curds, thick milk, seaweeds, nettles, stampy, 'mixed' bread and many other foods. This was an understandable feature of the sense of inferiority of people emerging from a great economic catastrophe, in our case the terrible famines, near-famines and depressions of the middle of the last century. Black forty-seven and the years after it left a very deep mark. But with the passing of the years we regain our confidence and nowadays many people are taking an interest in the old foods and are looking up their grandmothers' recipes and trying them out once more, and finding that many of them are worth trying.

Our Daily Bread

'Nua gacha bídh agus sean gacha dighe' says the Irish proverb, meaning that food should be eaten as fresh as possible while drink should be well-matured. This liking for fresh and freshly cooked food is one of the two main factors which have given us our traditional varieties of bread. The Irish housewife baked bread every day and was very apologetic when, by some mischance, she had to offer yesterday's bread to a guest. Often the bread was not baked until just before the meal and was eaten hot, and sometimes in harvest time the corn was reaped, the grain dried and ground into meal, and the bread kneaded, baked and eaten all on the same day. This was most often done with oats, and the threshing, winnowing and drying were, in an emergency, combined in the one swift and simple operation of burning the oats sheaf; the grain was then cleaned from the ashes and was ready for grinding in a quern. This 'burning in the sheaf' was so common at times that several laws were made against it, with the purpose of preventing the wastage of the useful straw.

But for the most part, the corn was ground in mills. Every parish had its mill, and some had several. All through the west and north the water mill was usual, while in parts of the south and east windmills were fairly common. South County Wexford was famous for the number of its windmills and the turning sails were a familiar feature of the landscape there a century ago,

Since people liked to have their bread freshly baked from recently ground flour, it was customary to store the grain, and have a sack or two ground as it was needed. Of course, Ireland always had enough water and wind to keep the wheels and the sails of the mills turning. Conditions in other countries might be quite different. In northern Scandinavia, for instance, small water mills were usual. But the dry summers often brought a drought, and there was a freeze-up all during the winter months, with the result that there was water enough to turn the mills only in Autumn and in Spring. So there was a big grinding of corn in the Autumn and again in the Spring and a great baking of kinds of bread which did not go stale. A six-months' supply was baked in the Autumn and stored away for use as required, and another half-year's supply was baked in the Spring to last until the following harvest. And a Swedish housewife was very apologetic if, by some mischance, she had to offer fresh bread to a guest, instead of bread well-matured in store. The bread baked for storage was usually made of rye or barley meal without any leaven. Some of it was as thin as a biscuit or even an ice-cream wafer. Often it was baked in round cakes with a hole in the middle, and then strung on ropes or rods and hung from the ceiling of the kitchen, as we used to hang flitches of bacon.

The other important factor in the origin of our traditional bread types is the cooking fire which determined the method of baking. In our case on the open hearth at floor level, without any permanent baking oven such as we find in other countries. In many parts of the Continent there is a large oven in every farmhouse, large enough to do sufficient bread for a week or more at one baking. In some areas this oven is part of the kitchen fireplace, while in others it is separate from it. Sometimes it is outside the house, standing by itself in a corner of the farmyard. When the oven is being used a hot fire is lit inside the oven itself and kept going until the brick lining is hot enough. Then the fire is taken out and the bread is put in to bake in the after-heat. The door is usually sealed up with clay or dough to make it quite airtight, and some types of bread are left inside until the oven has got quite cold – a matter of several hours. Ovens of this kind are almost unknown in Irish farmhouses. Some were used in larger farmhouses in parts of south Leinster and east Munster, but otherwise they were to be found only in the 'big houses' or in the village and town bakeries, which means that the ordinary Irish household in the countryside baked its bread in small quantities in some form of utensil on the open hearth.

Rye was used very little as a bread grain in Ireland. Barley was somewhat better known, but only in some barley growing districts. Wheat and oats, on the other hand, were commonly used for bread all over the country. It appears that wheat was always regarded as being better than oats, more palatable and more fashionable, and so oats has gradually fallen out of favour as material for making bread, and is now used only in a few places in the north. Bur formerly it was commonly used in every part of the country, and in some parts of Ulster and Connaught it was the ordinary everyday bread of whole counties, where wheaten bread was eaten only on very special occasions. And since they regarded wheaten bread as superior, people grew a little ashamed of the oaten bread and tried to get away from it. In the same way the white bread made by the town baker was, in many parts of the south, regarded as being in every way superior to the home-made kinds, and was always provided for important occasions. In some places it was considered indispensable to the visit of the clergy on 'station' days, and so was known as 'priest's bread'. This quite illogical but none the less powerful influence of fashion has led to the virtual disappearance of several kinds of bread formerly in use, and, indeed, has affected many aspects of our old traditions.

Oats bread was usually baked very thin and without any leaven; the finished article was about a quarter of an inch thick. The usual ingredients were oatmeal, salt and water, and the water was added hot so as to form a paste of the meal. It was rolled or patted out thin and baked leaning against a little stand in front of the fire. The 'hardening stands', as they were called, are common enough yet in some places, though seldom used now. Most of the survivors are made of iron, and are good blacksmith work, horseshoe shaped and about twelve or fifteen inches high. But wooden ones were common, too, and an improvised stand could be made in a few minutes from a triple-forked branch of a bush or a tree. A few handsomely made stone specimens are known from County Fermanagh, and a type that looked rather like a fender and held several cakes at the time was used in County Down. This oaten bread, of all the Irish breads, came nearest to the kinds made for storage in Scandinavia and elsewhere, for although people preferred to eat it fresh, it could be kept for weeks or months without becoming uneatable, and so it was favoured by travellers. Many an emigrant on his way to America in the old sailing ships carried a good bag of oats bread as his main food supply for the journey.

Griddle bread is another of the vanishing types. It appears that while oaten bread baked on the 'hardening stand' was the common kind in the west and north, griddle bread largely took its place in the east and south. Griddle bread is thin bread baked on a flat iron plate placed over the fire. Fifty years ago there was a griddle in every house in Munster, but how many are in use now? The griddle was a round iron plate, fifteen or eighteen inches in diameter. In most places they had two handles or 'ears', but County Wicklow went in for a type with only one handle. In most cases the griddle rested on a little trivet (three-legged stand) about four inches high, over a bed of glowing turf embers. The bread might be leavened or unleavened, but was always thin, say about half an inch thick. Half way through the baking the bread was turned over on the griddle, so that both sides were equally baked. Before baking the griddle cake was cut into four sections, or marked deeply with a cross so that it broke easily into four sections. The sections were called 'farls' in some places from an old word for a quarter, and 'pointers' in other places because of their shape. They were usually eaten hot from the griddle with butter melting into them. That this is an old custom is shown by an Englishman's account of Ireland in 1620, who wrote about bread thus – 'If you stay half an hower you shall have a cake of meale unboulted, and mingled with butter, baked on an yron called a girdle'.

The high point of Irish bread making is the soda bread

from the pot oven, deservedly recognised as one of the
finest bread types in the world. In spite of this, it seemed
doomed to extinction some years ago by the spread of
modern cooking methods and by the coming of the
motor bread vans into the farmers' yards. But its excellence has been recognized, and it is now firmly
established as the Irish bread *par excellence*.

Soda bread is, of course, leavened as its name implies,
the agent being bicarbonate of soda usually helped on
by sour milk. But in the past other leavens were used.
Yeast was one of these and another was barm obtained
from a brewery or made at home from potatoes. 'Sour
dough' was used, too. This was a method in which a
small portion of leavened dough was held over from the
baking and mixed into the next day's batch of dough
which was left stand for a time until the whole was leavened, and again a small portion of the dough was put
aside to leaven the next lot. In this way a fermentation
process could be kept active for a long period, even for
several years. In some places sour milk alone was used
to make the bread 'rise'.

The pot oven was a very good baking utensil. The
deep flat-bottomed pan with a closely fitting lid on
which glowing embers were piled to ensure even heating
gave perfect results in baking, and skill in baking was a
countrywoman's pride and one of her chief claims to
good housewifery. This too, is in keeping with ancient
tradition. The English word 'lady' originally meant
'bread maker', and in the ancient laws of Ireland,
formulated over a thousand years ago, the sign of a
woman's right and dignity consisted of the bread making
utensils, the sieve, losset and griddle.

Tradition tells of other kinds of bread and other methods of baking now obsolete. We hear of bread laid directly, or protected by a cabbage leaf, on the embers, to bake. A well-known method was to make a small hot fire on the 'flag of the hearth', then move it aside, wipe the flag clean and lay the bread directly on it: when the time came to turn the cake, another part of the flagstone had been heated, and the cake was turned on to that. We hear of the use of peas and beans for bread, and there were, of course, the 'stampy' and 'boxty' and other kinds made from cooked and mashed potatoes or from raw grated potatoes from which the liquid had been squeezed out. And there were several kinds of 'mixed' bread, made from mixtures of different flours and meals in varying proportions, oats and wheat, or flour and potatoes, or one of the really fine bread types, griddle cakes of wheat flour and maize meal. A 'pointer' of this 'yalla male mixed bread' hot from the griddle and running with butter and a mug of new milk made a meal worth getting hungry for.

What did they Drink?

There is plenty of evidence to show that our ancestors, from the most remote times, were just as fond of a drop of drink as are their descendants to-day. Indeed, it seems that at most times in the past people drank a good deal more than they do now. In the ancient Irish literature there are many descriptions of banquets at which both men and women sat to table drinking off cup after cup and frequently raising their voices in song. We are not told if they all sang the same song at the same time, but that it sounded sweet to themselves is shown by the fact that the modern Irish word for a concert meant 'ale-music' in ancient times.

Nor did they always rise sober from the table. One old tale tells of a banquet in Ulster at which a hundred barrels of ale were drunk, the effect of which was that the Ulstermen found themselves disturbing the peace of Munster before they recovered their senses. On another occasion when the High King, Cathair Mór, and all his courtiers lay in a drunken sleep after the celebration of Samhain a thief slipped in and stole the golden crown off the Queen's head, for it appears that Her Majesty was just as intoxicated as any of them. Naturally such conduct met with disapproval at times, at least. Once upon a time when Saint Patrick was travelling through Connaught he was visited by a certain king who appeared before him sadly in liquor. The Saint was far from pleased at this discourtesy and foretold that all the king's descendants would be drunkards and, without exception, come to a bad end. And so it came to pass.

In those far off days the commonest drink was ale. Anyone who wished to do so was allowed to brew ale for his own use, but the ancient laws laid down regulations for the brewing of ale for sale, and for the proper running of alehouses, as well as fines for drunkenness. Sometimes the ale was drunk hot, and often it was flavoured with spice. Ale was drunk in the monasteries too, and it was ordered that, at a feast, laymen and clerics got equal quantities of food, but the laymen got twice as much ale as the clerics. Saint Patrick himself, though he might reprove a drunken king, had a brewer in his own household, and Saint Brighid was praised for the excellence of the ale she brewed.

Even in ancient times there was a considerable trade in wine with the Continent. Furs and hides were exported from Ireland to Gaul and cargoes of wine came back in return, so that wine was a well-known drink, at least in the houses of the great. Once when the High King, Muircheartach Mac Earca, was entertaining his chieftains and warriors the palace was set on fire, and the king, in trying to escape the flames, jumped into a barrel of wine and was drowned in it. It appears that some attempts were made by the monks to grow the vine for the making of altar-wine, but without success because of the climate.

Another favourite drink was mead, which appears to have been regarded as a great delicacy. It was made from honey. It seems that bees were kept in very great numbers in ancient times, much more so than now, for honey was widely used for sweetening and flavouring as the manufacture of sugar was unknown in Western Europe. To have a surplus of honey for mead-making was highly praised, and districts which produced mead in quantity were lauded by the poets.

For the most part these beverages were drunk from wooden cups or bowls. But there is mention of fine cups of silver, bronze and gold, some of which must have been very handsome, if we are to judge from the Ardagh Chalice which is one of the most beautiful objects ever made. We read, too, of cups of glass and of the horns of cattle and even of buffaloes made into drinking vessels, and of large nut shells from the 'Eastern World' which must have been something like gourds or coconuts. We need not be surprised at the buffalo horns or the coconuts, for, after all, several products of the Orient, for instance pepper and silk, were well-known in ancient Ireland.

Milk was drunk in many forms. Fresh milk, of course, and skimmed milk, as nowadays. But there were many varieties of sour milk. And these were not the accidental product of milk turned sour by mischance, although we can be sure that that did not go to waste either. There were certain ways of making fresh milk sour. It might be poured into a vessel which had already held sour milk, or have some sour milk or cream added to it. Or certain substances, such as rennet or butterwort might be added to it. Or it might be broken into curds and whey, and the whey drunk. For people had learned that there were many ways of making milk sour, and that different methods produced drinks of different taste. In hotels in Norway and Sweden you may see two or three tureens on the sideboard of the dining-room, each with different kind of sour milk, from which the diners help themselves, and beside the tureens are dishes of sugar, ginger, cinnamon and other flavourings to add to the sour milk according to each person's taste. If we had held to our old customs more firmly we might see the same in Irish hotels to-day. In dealing with sour milk we must not forget the by-product of the churn, buttermilk, which was another favourite drink as long as butter was churned at home, and a renowned thirst quencher on a hot summer's day. Buttermilk varied, too, according to what was put in the churn; sweet cream gave one kind, and sour cream another, while the putting of whole milk in the churn gave still another. The old people say that quarts of buttermilk could be drunk without ill effect, and tell many a tale of buttermilk drinking contests at which gallons were drunk by each competitor.

Whiskey is of comparatively recent origin. Nobody can say when the art of distilling was introduced into Ireland, but the first mention of whiskey comes from the year 1405, when an annalist wrote of the sad fate of one Richard Mac Raghnaill who was the heir to a property in south County Leitrim and who died from drinking *uisce beatha*. 'Water of life' said the annalist 'but it was water of death for Richard'.

But, in spite of the lesson on the evils of the abuse of strong drink given by the demise of Richard, voices were raised on all sides in praise of the 'Water of Life'. Foreigners marvelled at its potency and its flavour, while the natives of the country continued to drink it. By the time that the first Elizabeth came to the throne of England, Irish whiskey was already famous. During her reign one Englishman wrote 'The Irish aqua vitae, commonly called usquebaugh, is held the best in the world of that kind; it is made also in England, but nothing so good as that which is brought out of Ireland. And the usquebaugh is preferred before our aqua vitae, because the mingling of raisins, fennel-seed and other things mitigating the heat, and making the taste pleasant, make it less inflame, and yet refresh the weak stomach with moderate heat and a good relish'. Apparently it was usual to flavour the whiskey, as another Englishman tells us 'It is sweetened with liquorice, made potable, and is of the colour of Muscadine. It is a very wholesome drink, and natural to digest the crudities of the Irish feeding. You may drink a naggin without offence.' This custom of adding herbs or flavourings to whiskey is now almost completely dead in Ireland, but in other countries people still buy quantities of the local spirits, schnaps or brännvin, and bottle it, adding to each bottle some substance which improves the flavour or the colour or gives it a curative quality. Some of the things added to the spirits are blackberries, whortleberries, cherries, caraway seeds, cowslips, sloes, black currants, aniseed, elderberries, elder flowers, camomile, lily of the valley, wormwood, tansy, yarrow, thyme, rosemary, angelica and lavender flowers, and there are dozens of others.

A couple of hundred years ago hot drinks were all the fashion. There was mulled ale and porter, punch, hot spiced wine, possets, buttered whisky or rum, and *scáiltín*, which was a blend of hot milk, butter, sugar and whiskey, flavoured with cinnamon or cloves; this could be powerful as well as pleasant, especially when the whiskey was the product of someone's homework. Both French and Spanish wines were very popular, too, and quite a lot of brandy was drunk. And a lot of the imported drink never saw a customs official, for smuggling was common all along the coast. The boats that took the Wild Geese to France seldom came back without a carge of casks to be landed in a quiet cove on a dark night, often with the help of the local landlord who got as his 'cut' a cask of wine and a bolt of silk for his lady.

It is only during the last couple of hundred years that tea and coffee came into anything like general use. Coffee was the first to come, and for a time it seemed that it would become the ordinary drink of the people, as it has in France and Spain and most of the countries of Western Europe. But history takes some queer turns. Britain and France fought for the mastery of India and Britain won, bringing the trade of the East under British control, and a market must be found for the great tea production of India and China, so the drinking of tea was encouraged at the expense of coffee. And so a war fought ten thousand miles away two hundred years ago decided what we drink at our breakfasts. When that war was fought coffee cost one and tenpence a pound in Ireland, while tea was eleven or twelve shillings. A hundred years later coffee was still about the same price but tea had come down to three shillings a pound.

And so times change. If we were transported back to ancient Ireland, it is probable that the only drink familiar to us would be fresh milk. The same would be true of the time of Queen Elizabeth. Of course there always was the poor man's drink – fresh water. But what would we make of mead or 'usquebaugh' flavoured with liquorice? Or what, for that matter, would King Cormac Mac Airt or our friend Richard, the first recorded victim of whiskey, make of Gaelic Coffee?

Mountain Dew

The talk in the pub turned, as sooner or later it always does, to the price of the drink and, as usual, our local historian had something to say. 'It was Cromwell, the old wretch, that started it. It wasn't enough for him to massacre the citizens in Drogheda and Wexford and hunt the priests like wolves and drive people to Hell and Connaught. The devil had to pinch him to put a tax on the whiskey too. Excise is what he called it – the same word the doctor uses when he cuts a bit out of you.' Our friend's information was not quite exact, but nearly so; it was the English Parliament in revolt against the King which first collected excise in the 1640s, copying the Dutch. The idea was too good to drop, and the restored monarch, Charles II, chronically hard-up, continued the good work and extended it to Ireland. And henceforth not only were drinks dearer but the small private distiller plied his trade only by either paying up or living in fear of the law.

Irish whiskey had been famous for long years before this and visitors to Ireland were loud in its praise. Anybody who wished could set up a still and go into business. Every castle and mansion and every inn could have its own particular extract and all sorts of wonderful blends and flavourings were to be had. Then came the laws which demanded licenses and the payment of duty, and with them the illicit distillers.

At first the laws were enforced only in the towns and

more settled parts of the country. The duty was small, only 4d. a gallon at first, and only a shilling or so a gallon by the time of Grattan's parliament in the 1780s. Whiskey made with the Government's blessing was very little dearer than the home-made product, and for those farmers within reach of the distilleries the market for grain was good. On the other hand the law hardly penetrated into the remote west and north of the country and the poitín stills flourished there. The local magnates winked at it. Many a landlord knew that much of the rents paid to him came from the making of poitín or from the sale of barley and oats to the illicit distillers. Moreover, the old skill and care were still practised and the home-made spirit was often of much better quality and flavour than that of the town distilleries. And while the landlords and gentry who lived on their rents and loved a good drop were also the local law officers and magistrates the poitín makers ran very little risk of being disturbed. Some of the gentry, indeed, has stills set up in their own houses and most of them had a pet poitín maker to supply their wants.

Good poitín needed the greatest care in its making. First the grain, barley or a mixture of barley and oats, had to be malted by soaking in water until it swelled; the malt was then spread out on a clean surface to sprout and carefully turned over twice a day to ensure evenness. Everything must be clean and fresh as the least thing might taint the malt and spoil the whole process. After ten or twelve days of this the grain was dried in a kiln and ground into meal. Next the meal was put in a big tub and boiling water was poured upon it. When it cooled some yeast was added to start fermentation and the liquid was put into barrels and left stand for about four weeks. Then it was put in the still and distilled, the product of the first 'run' being a raw spirit very useful for removing tar stains or massaging rheumatic limbs but scarcely fit for drinking. It had to be distilled a second time. This gave raw poitín. Some enthusiasts ran it through the still a third time to make a very potent but very palatable whiskey. Whether distilled twice or three times the spirit needed to be matured for a while – for months or even years – to bring it to its best, and for this maturing a cask which had contained wine was thought best. Thus the whole production took many weeks and needed not only skill and care, but freedom from interruption too.

Then came Napoleon's wars. The market for corn of all kinds improved and the poitín trade might have died a natural death if the rates of duty on all sorts of products, including spirits, had not soared until three quarters of the price of a drink want in taxes. This led to a revival of the illicit trade and an intensification of the Government's efforts to put it down. Open war waged in many places between the 'gaugers' and the distillers, with firearms freely used on both sides. Often parties of soldiers were sent out to aid the preventive men, and had to struggle along in their bright red tight-fitting coats with heavy muskets and packs through mountains and bogs. The whole countryside was in sympathy with the poitín men. The redcoats could be seen miles away. Often they were misled by 'friendly natives' and directed along paths which led into bog-holes or deep streams. Or the leading file stepped into a carefully covered pitfall and found himself up to his neck in dirty water. Or a nimble long-legged mount-aineer ran out before them carrying a suspicious-looking keg and the chase continued for miles across the roughest country, until finally the quarry threw down the keg which was found to contain only a few dregs of tar or tallow and not a smell of poitín. All of which was retold with trimmings by the delighted country people, and a good time was had by all except the unfortunate soldiers. But the poitín maker and his product both suffered from this harrying. Gone were the leisurely days when all care and skill could be lavished on the process, and the finished spirit sank in quality and in general esteem.

Then came the final blow, the establishment of the Royal Irish Constabulary. When all is said and done the R.I.C. was a fine body of men, big strong fellows, mostly the sons of small farmers, well-trained and disciplined. If Government stupidity had not made them the enemies of the ordinary people by using them to repress political freedom and bolster up the crumbling landlord system they might have turned out to be as good and beneficial a police force as any in the world. Whatever their other activities they never ceased their campaign against the poitín men, and since they knew the countryside and its people so well they were not to be taken in by the crude tricks that had baffled the soldiers and the 'gaugers'. They made the illicit distillers' life a misery and the quality of the poitín grew worse and worse until it was despised by most people, even by hardened drinkers.

Not that the 'peelers' always had it their own way. There were remote glens and islands, difficult to ap-proach without being seen in time to store everything safely away, and in such places the trade went on. Once,

after many days on the lookout, the police swooped
down on an island in Lough Corrib. They knew the old
trick of sinking the still and the barrels in the lake with a
rope attached, and after long searching found several
ropes well hidden, but these when hauled in brought
dead dogs and other smelly and unpleasant objects to the
surface. On another occasion a sergeant and a constable
found a twenty gallon keg full of prime poitín in the loft
over the lower room of a Mayo farmhouse. The constable was sent off to bring reinforcements while the
sergeant sat solidly on the keg with his carbine across his
knees and refused to be distracted by odd noises made by
the women in the room below. The men, naturally, had
disappeared on the approach of the limbs of the law. A
couple of hours later a side-car arrived with four con-
stables, but the keg when lifted came up light as a
feather. The woman had carefully bored through the
loft floor and the bottom of the keg with an auger and
drawn off the poitín. Not even the smell remained, for
they had thoughtfully squirted a couple of pints of
paraffin oil up into the empty keg. No evidence meant
no conviction, and the 'peelers' had to retreat in no very
sweet temper.

A careful watch was kept by the police on all grain
grown in the poitín districts, and the growers had to
account for it. This made poitín making still more
difficult, and by the end of the nineteenth century all
sorts of poor substitutes for the good clean malt had come
into use. We hear of pig-meal, raw grain, potatoes, sugar,
treacle, even sawdust, and all sorts of mixtures of these,
with unlikely substances such as bluestone, carbide,
sulphuric acid and soap being added to pep the mixture

up, so that the end product was often a danger to health and sanity. And the good copper stills of the eighteenth century were no longer seen; makeshifts banged together from sheet tin had taken their place, with tar-cans, old milk tankards or oil drums instead of the clean casks made by the old time coopers. An ancient skilled craft had degenerated into a crude, dirty, unwholesome botch, condemned by church, state and the public at large.

We may wonder what might have developed if the authorities, instead of repressing local distillation had found some method of fostering it. It might have grown into a valuable home industry with a large variety of fine liqueurs as it has in some European countries. In the early part of the last century poitín making was hardly known in Leinster, Munster or east Ulster, the more prosperous areas of Ireland, but well-known and widely practised in Connaught and west Ulster where an established home industry might have been very valuable. But it is easy to be wise after the event, and it is to be feared that the ancient craft has gone the way of so many of the old traditional skills.

Tobacco

On last Saint Stephen's Day, on a quiet country road,
I met a group of Wren Boys resplendent in their sashes
and ribbons, complete with fiddle, flute and *bodhrán*.
And gripped between the teeth of every man of them
was a large cigar. They had just come from the house of
a jovial gentleman who was so pleased with their enter-
tainment that he had insisted on passing round a box
that had come to him a few days before as a Christmas
present. Leaving them to pursue their Havana-scented
way, I betook me to the shop at the cross-roads, there to
lay my finger on the pulse of the parish. Had she any
cigars for sale? 'Cigars, is it? Indeed I have, though 'tis
little I thought when I used be helping my father to
pack the Christmas presents for the customers, and
putting a half-quarter of plug into many a one of them
that I'd see the day I'd be selling cigars like any of the
big shops above in Grafton Street. 'Twas the returned
Yanks, I suppose, or maybe them that's home from
England that started it. But sure –' waving towards the
shelves loaded with canned and packaged goods '– 'tis
all new things we're selling now. But of course 'tis only
around Christmas that there's much call on cigars.'

I could see her point. My mind went back to the days
when she used to fill out *tóisíns* of sweets to us from a
big jar, and when her stock in trade was made up of
sides of bacon and strings of onions, great rolls of plug
tobacco and tins of snuff, bunches of ribbons, bootlaces

and 'gallusses', and boxes, bins and bags full of groceries to be weighed out in paper bags. The local wags often said that her mother – who was short in the sight – often cut the bacon, the butter, the onions and the tobacco all with the same knife. 'Of course, you might hardly notice it in the onions, and it didn't matter much in the tobacco!' was their verdict on the result of this economy of appliances. And now, cigars. Times are changing without a doubt.

But, although they are new to that good lady and that quiet countryside, we are told that the first time ever that men of Europe saw tobacco in use it was in the form of cigars. When Columbus landed in the West Indies a local chieftain wished to do him honour and solemnly presented him with a small roll of dried leaves and an elegant little forked stick with which to hold it. Columbus, no doubt, smiled and tried to hide his ignorance of what it was, but the chieftain set a live coal to one end of the little roll and drew heartily on the other, emitting clouds of fragrant smoke from his mouth and nostrils. 'Tabago!' quoth the chieftain, flourishing the forked cigar holder. Other explorers up the Saint Lawrence and the Orinoco, in Virginia and Mexico and Florida, saw the same wonder and learned the use of cigars, pipes and snuff, and soon it was the fashion of the courts and the seaport towns of Europe.

Its reception was a mixed one. Fashionable young men thought highly of it, while sailors and soldiers flaunted their pipes as symbols of their distant landfalls and foreign wars. But authority, both civil and ecclesiastical, spoke out against it. Bishops waxed wrathful at snuffing in church. King James the First of England

wrote a pamphlet against it – 'A Counterblaste to
Tabacco'. The King of France forbade its use in any
form. As far afield as Russia and India and Japan there
were edicts and proclamations against it. It seemed as if
the new fashion of 'drinking smoke' was doomed. But in
spite of all the laws of state and all the fulminations of
churchmen the habit spread and spread, through
Europe, through Asia, through Africa, graining ground
every year. The medical fraternity noted its soothing
effect and prescribed it widely for all manner of ailments,
and it was easy to find some pain or ache to excuse an
occasional whiff or pinch. Then some financial genius
in government circles had a brainwave – why not turn
this madness to good account by clapping a tax on
tobacco? This did the trick. The devotees of the weed
were not averse to a few pence extra on the cost, and
the resulting flow of ready cash into the state funds
gradually stilled the chorus of disapproval. Smoking had
come to stay.

We all have heard the story of the first coming of
tobacco to Ireland, how Sir Walter Raleigh sat at ease
in his garden in Youghal, smoking his pipe and dreaming of further piratical raids, when his new servant boy,
terrified at the cloud of smoke, 'quinched' him with a big
pail of water. In his breezy account of Ireland in 1620,
Justice Luke Gernon extols the hospitality of the
castles... 'the fyre is prepared in the middle of the hall,
where you may sollace yourselfe till supper time – you
shall not want sacke and tobacco'. Eighty years later an
English traveller, Dunton, marvelled to find tobacco
in common use in the remotest part of Connaught. He
need not have been surprised; at the time there were

severe laws against direct importation of tobacco into Ireland – it had first to be landed in England, to pay tax there – and the Conamara men were expert smugglers. A hundred and fifty years ago another traveller remarked with heavy disapproval that not only all the boys but many of the girls of fourteen years or so were pipe smokers, while the sophisters, economists and calculators of the early nineteenth century, seeking to solve on paper all the ills of Ireland, were loud in their complaints that the 'common labourers' spent as much as a halfpenny a day on tobacco! Incidentally, the old people used to say that you'd get 'as much as would go round your waist of rat's tail twist for twopence', so a halfpennyworth wasn't such a bad smoke.

Smoking and snuffing was especially popular at wakes. This may have come from a notion that tobacco protected the living from the ailment that had carried off the dead person. Whatever the reason – and it may have been merely a show of hospitality – everyone coming to the wakehouse, young or old, gentle or simple, must smoke a pipe or take a pinch of snuff. New clay pipes, ready filled, were laid out in dozens, and a large plate of snuff lay by the corpse. And everybody smoked or snuffed with a prayer for the dead – a custom that was extended to all smoking and snuffing, for the old people always said 'Lord have mercy on the souls of the dead!' whenever they lit up or took a pinch. Many tales are told about this custom. There is the well-known story of the man who came upon a ghost smoking a pipe. The ghost offered him the pipe, and he took it with a prayer for the dead. Again it was offered and again he prayed, and again a third time. Then the ghost spoke; no one had ever prayed for him, and he could not gain Heaven without the prayers of a living Christian, but now he was accepted in Heaven, and the man could keep the pipe which never would need to be refilled as long as he told nobody where it came from. Of course he couldn't keep his mouth shut, and so the pipe lost its power, but we gained a good story.

Then there were the two old ladies walking home one winter's night and regretting that they had no light for their pipes, and lo ! there on the churchyard wall was a glowing coal. They lit up with fervent prayers for those who lay in the churchyard, and left the coal burning on the wall. Then came a tinker who never said any prayers, and as he stretched his hand for the coal, the fire went out of it and it was dead and cold.

'Twist' was the commonest form of tobacco in former times. The leaves were damped and twisted into a thin rope, and this was secured at intervals with string and left to mature before use. It was usually sold by length rather than by weight. Once upon a time Daniel O'Connell won a case for a client, a sailor, against a shopkeeper, and prompted the client to ask, as damages, 'as much twist as would reach from the sole of his foot to the tip of his ear'. When the shopkeeper agreed to what seemed to be a token payment it was revealed to him that the tip of the sailor's ear had been cut off in a knife brawl in a South American seaport years before, and he was glad to pay a hundred pounds to escape the impossible task of providing so much tobacco. Men usually carried a tinder box containing a flint and steel, and a piece of tinder – usually charred linen rags – to catch the spark struck from the flint. One of the most usual callers at any house beside the road was the man who wanted a light for his pipe, and such a caller was always permitted to take a live coal or a bogdeal splinter from the fire and light up before going on his way. But if the churn was being made, he was not to leave the house until the butter came, for fear he might steal away the profit of the churn. And if it happened to be May Eve he must smoke the pipe out before leaving the house, for fire taken out of a house on that day could be used to the detriment of the inhabitants of that house.

Possibly because pipes may have seemed out of place in the elegant drawing-rooms of the eighteenth century gentry, the taking of snuff became very much the rage among the fashionable gentlemen of the time. Handsome snuff boxes of jewelled or enamelled gold or silver were freely flourished, and a fine specimen might be the present of a grateful king or prince to a deserving subject. Young gentlemen were taught the finer points of taking snuff with a graceful air, and to be offered a pinch from the box of a mighty lord or famous statesman was an honour much sought after by the social climbers of the day. Elderly ladies, too, were partial to snuff. There were many different kinds and grades of snuff to be had, from light and perfumed mixtures for beginners to dark and explosive compounds for the seasoned devotee. At the other end of the social scale was chewing tobacco, looked down upon by the snuffers as a low and beastly habit, but especially favoured by sailors. Smoking, except at certain times and in safe parts of the ship was usually forbidden in both naval and merchant services, for the old wooden ships, reeking with tar, were highly inflammable, and a fire at sea was a dreadful calamity.

But the men on watch or at the wheel were, by long standing custom, permitted to chew tobacco provided they did not spit on the deck. Nowadays we hardly ever see tobacco being chewed, except by a few old sailors and fishermen.

Cigarettes are the newest form of 'smoke'. In parts of Spanish America, especially in Mexico, they have been popular for centuries – they were and still are rolled by hand, often not in paper but in the silky inner husk of maize. But it is less than a hundred years since they came into this part of the world; indeed the first cigarette making machines were invented as recently as 1880. Now they are the commonest form and millions are smoked every day, as eagerly by women as by men. Many of us remember pipes being smoked by old ladies of our acquaintance, but you never see a young woman with a pipe, although all things are possible in a world where fashions change so quickly, and who knows what a few years may bring?

And what about our cigars? Still the commonest form of 'smoke' in their ancestral home, the West Indies, they were, until recently, a mark of luxury and opulence here. Hence we regard them as suitable to the special occasion, and hence the Christmas cigar which was such a source of wonder to my old friend in the shop at the cross roads. And although they are still a man's prerogative, we hear an occasional rumour that this preserve, too, is being invaded.

The American Indians gave to the world three plants which have become of vast importance, potatoes, maize and tobacco. By a strange turn of fate two of these, in Ireland, are associated with the 'bad times', with memories of the potato crop failures and their resultant famines, with 'yalla male' being doled out to relieve the hungry. But tobacco has become a solace and a luxury for rich and poor alike. And while maize and potatoes belong to the sphere of practical economics, tobacco has drawn about it a large body of belief, custom, tale and legend.

What did they Wear?

We can learn a lot about the clothes worn by our ancestors a thousand years ago or more. There are pictures in some of the illuminated manuscripts like the Book of Kells, carvings of people on ancient churches and crosses, descriptions of the dress of the chieftains and ladies in the old literature and all the bits of cloth, leather and metal found by chance or dug up by the archaeologists. All of these fit together to give us a fairly clear idea of what was worn in Ireland before the Normans came.

For men there were two quite different forms of dress. The first was worn by people of rank and dignity, by nobles, priests and professional men such as lawyers, poets, doctors and others whose age or wealth or social position required stately clothes. This consisted of two main garments, a long tunic with sleeves and an opening for the head, put on like a shirt and reaching to half way down the shin. The second garment, a long sleeveless cloak fitted to the shoulders, was worn over the tunic; the cloak reached to the knee and could be worn loosely or wrapped tight and fastened with a large brooch or pin.

The second form of dress was worn by young men and those who followed strenuous and active pursuits, such as farmers, soldiers, hunters and so on. It was made up of two main garments, a pair of tightly fitting trousers and a short jacket. In some cases the trousers were like a footballer's shorts, others were fastened below the knee, like knee-breeches, and others reached the ankle and had a strap under the instep.

Women wore a long dress reaching to the ankles and a cloak like that of the men; indeed there was little difference between the dress of the women and that of the men of position, except in style, cut, materials, colours and so on. As to materials, both wool and linen were common, wool for cloaks and for rough wear and linen for tunics. Silk was known and worn on fine occasions, while active and hardworking men wore garments of skin or leather. Bright colours were popular. The old literature mentions red, blue, purple, green, grey, white, black and yellow, and tells of patterned materials and of embroidery, borders, stripes and fringes... especially on cloaks. The long tunics, and the women's dresses, were often made of white linen with applied or embroidered decoration in gold and various bright colours.

Although we read of shoes and sandals of leather, some of them dyed and decorated, it appears that these were kept for special occasions, and that most people went barefoot nearly all the time. There is some mention, too, of hats and caps, but the usual headgear was a hood attached to the cloak, or a fold of the cloak draped over the head.

The coming of the Normans brought little change, except in minor points of changing fashion. Elder and dignified men still wore the long tunic and cloak, while the younger and active wore the jacket-and-trousers. Women continued to wear a long dress and a cloak.

The National Museum has a man's suit, found in a bog in County Sligo, which was made about five hundred years ago, and is a good example of what the ordinary man wore at that period. There are three garments, a jacket, a pair of trousers and a cloak. The jacket reached to the knee; it fitted closely to the body as far as the waist and had a very full skirt. It opens down the front with fourteen buttons. The sleeves have an open seam on the under side all the way up to the armpit, fastening with twelve buttons on each sleeve, so that it might be closed about the arm or allowed to hang open. The trousers fitted tightly to the legs and reached the feet. The cloak is of semicircular shape, like a cyclist's cape. It has no sleeves and hung down to the wearer's shins. All these three garments are made of homespun woollen material. The cloak and the jacket are of a brown colour but the legs of the trousers have a criss-cross pattern of brown stripes on a lighter brown background. Of course the original colours have been affected by the bog.

The long tunic was still worn by many men, but it was often drawn up and secured by a belt so that it hung about to the knee. Often, now, a pair of trousers was worn under it. The sleeves of the tunic were tight at the shoulder but very loose and flowing about the lower arm. Many men wore short jackets of cloth or leather over the tunic; some of these jackets were decorated with applied or embroidered patterns. The jacket sleeves opened along the under side, so that the flowing tunic sleeves could hang down. Soldiers wore a very heavy tunic which was well padded or quilted and reached down to the knee. This saved the man's body from the chafing of his heavy chain-armour and absorbed some of the shock of blows in battle.

By the later years of the sixteenth century, the time of

Queen Elizabeth's wars in Ireland, the long tunic
tucked up under the belt had developed into a regular
shirt skirted with a very elaborate array of pleats, and
these shirts, worn over a pair of tight trousers, became
the usual men's dress. An Englishman who was in
Ireland in 1581 wrote

'Their shirts be very strange
Not reaching past the thigh;
With pleats on pleats they pleated are
As thick as pleats may lie.'

The fashionable colour for the shirt was saffron. We
should note that saffron was made from the flower of the
Autumn Crocus (specially grown for dye making) and
was a pure bright daffodil yellow without any trace of
brown, quite different from the muddy brown colour
now often called saffron. Some men wore tight fitting
leather jackets or jerkins over their shirts, but the shirt
sleeves continued to be very full and sweeping, and this
bright yellow shirt, with its remarkable pleating and its
hanging sleeves was regarded as the typically Irish dress
by people from abroad. The other, and even more
typically Irish, men's garment was the great cloak,
which seems to have changed very little down the
centuries. Made from strong woollen material it was
often dyed a bright colour and usually had a fringe of
another colour all around the edge; some of them had a
collar of sheepskin or fur at the neck. Many had a curly
pile brought up on the outside of the woollen cloth;
often they were lined with finer material. They were
splendid garments, much sought after even outside of
Ireland. In the year 1504 two thousand three hundred
and twenty of these Irish cloaks were exported to

Bristol. Their fine qualities brought them under the ban of the law, because their use enabled the Irish fighting men to remain out in the hills and woods in the worst of weather. They were still worn by the Irish soldiers who fought against Cromwell. The regiment of Colonel Philip MacHugh O'Reilly, which had fought gallantly at the siege of Clonmel went to the Continent after the war in Ireland had been lost, and continued to wear their Irish dress 'in foreign service. 'Strong, big-boned, sinewy, very brave men, born fighters and by now veterans, dressed in the old Irish fashion of tight trousers and cloaks down to their heels, many of the cloaks of variegated colours' is a description of this regiment fighting in Belgium.

An English judge who lived in Limerick wrote an account of things in Ireland about the year 1620. He has a long description of the dress of the women. About hats he says that in Kilkenny 'broad beaver hats coloured, edged with gold lace and faced with velvet' were the fashion. In Waterford it was 'caps turned up with fur and laced with gold lace'. In Limerick they wore 'rolls of linen, made up in the form of a mitre'. In Connaught the ladies wore 'rolls in the form of a cheese' and in Thomond 'kerchiefs hanging down to the middle of their backs'. There was no lack of variety in the fashions of those days. He mentions, too, that the unmarried girls decorated their plaited hair with about four yards of coloured ribbon. He tells of necklaces, rings and bracelets, of silk scarves and silver buttons, wide skirts, waistcoats and laced bodices, satin sleeves and silk waist belts with hanging tassels, knitted stockings of various colours. Of their cloaks he says 'They wear their mantles also as well within doors as without. Their mantles are commonly of a brown-blue colour with fringe alike, but those that love to be gallant wear them of green, red, yellow, and other light colours with fringes diversified'.

A woman's dress, found in a bog in County Tipperary, and preserved in the National Museum, may belong to this period. It consists of a bodice and a skirt joined together. The bodice is open down the front to show a vest or blouse worn underneath. The skirt is very full and voluminous, being made up of no less than ninety-two gores, each two inches wide at the top and three at the bottom, the sewing of which must have taken many days of work. This skirt measures over twenty-two feet around the lower edge.

Several different kinds of men's headgear are known from this period, and the wearing of shoes by both men and women had become common, although it is probable that poorer people always went barefoot, while even the more prosperous laid aside their shoes at times.

During the hundred years from 1650 to 1750, the distinctive dress of the Irish men was laid aside, and the ordinary fashion of the time taken in its place. This finished the wearing of the bright yellow shirt and the cloak. Women's dress, however, did not change much. In the main it was made up of a tight bodice and a full skirt, while the great cloak developed into the hooded cloak worn in some parts of the country down to our own time.

During the period of Grattan's Parliament and the Wars of Napoleon comparative prosperity reigned in Ireland. There were good prices for all kinds of produce and everybody had a few shillings to jingle in his pocket. Most people could afford to buy good new clothes, and the men's new suits were modelled on the fashion of the horse-riding gentlemen of the time, tightly fitting knee breeches and a tail coat. The breeches were usually made of brown or yellow corduroy and the coat of homespun or broadcloth of fairly bright colours such as plum, brown, grey, bottle green or dark or light blue. Knitted stockings of brown, grey, blue or white wool were worn, and shirts of white linen with a bright cravat. Young men who wished to cut a dash wore brightly coloured and patterned waistcoats, with brass or silver buttons on their coats and at the knees of the breeches which were fastened outside the stockings and so showed off the buttons. Low cut black shoes and a tall hat completed the picture, and both hat and shoes were set off with brass or even silver buckles. This form of dress continued in use in most parts of Ireland for the greater part of the nineteenth century, and almost became the Irishman's national dress.

All during the nineteenth century the hooded cloak was the Irishwoman's characteristic garment. A few may still be seen worn by older women in parts of County Cork; these are of a sober black, but a hundred years ago many of the cloaks were brightly coloured, red, pale or dark grey, bottle green, various shades of light and dark blue. In parts of the west cloaks of creamy coloured undyed woollen material were worn; other parts of the country, too, favoured cloaks of homespun material, but most women preferred fine broadcloth; the cloak was an expensive item of dress, but it lasted for many years and was always in fashion. Often the inside was lined with satin of a contrasting or matching colour. The hood was worn on the head or lying on the shoulders; married women usually wore a white frilled cap under it.

In the course of the nineteenth century as the cloak was laid aside a cheaper substitute for it was found in the shawl which now, in its turn, is yielding to the changing fashion. Young women liked to wear bright stockings, white, grey, red or sky blue, with low cut black shoes; their skirts came to about half-way down the shin, so that pretty ankles were duly admired. The fitted bodice and wide skirt continued to be worn. In the earlier years of the nineteenth century necks were cut low, but in the later years of the century high necks came into fashion. The skirts were usually dyed madder red, but indigo, various shades of blue, apple and pea green and brown and grey were also worn. On fine occasions a gown of light material, such as cotton, was worn over the bodice-and-skirt, and looped up to show the darker skirt underneath. Often the bodice was of a different colour or shade to the skirt, and both skirt and bodice might be trimmed with bands of dark velvet.

On parts of the west coast men wore wide trousers, sailor fashion, or tighter trousers slit or gored at the outer side of the lower leg; this was to permit them to be pulled up over the knee. Heavy fishermen's jerseys were commonly worn by coast dwellers, and a double breasted waistcoat with braided edges was worn over the jersey. In the south-west a waistcoat with sleeves was often worn instead of a coat. The loose *bainín* jacket, a very fine working garment, has only recently been discarded in favour of surplus military tunics. Another working garment was a heavy shirt of the same undyed *bainín*, worn over a lighter shirt of linen. The men of the coast preferred a low-crowned, wide-brimmed, black hat to the 'caroline' worn generally inland. Around Galway Bay boys wore a knitted cap with a woollen bob, and the *crios*, the woven woollen waistbelt of the Aran fishermen has come well into fashion in recent years.

During the last sixty or seventy years there has been a movement in most of the countries of Europe to keep in use, as a dress for festive occasions, the old local or provincial costumes of both men and women. People talk of 'folk-dress' and 'national costume' and are very eager to learn about them and wear them. With such a wealth of interesting and beautiful forms of dress worn in Ireland in the past it seems a very great pity that the form of dress believed by many to be Irish was invented about sixty years ago, in the early days of the Gaelic revival, and is quite bogus. The so called 'Irish kilt' is merely a copy of the Scottish kilt, taken over in the belief that both Irish and Scots must have worn it at some former time. In actual fact the kilt was never an Irish dress, and, although there is nothing to prevent men and boys wearing a Scottish form of dress if they wish to do so, it is quite wrong to claim it as an 'Irish National Costume'.

As to a 'national dress' for women and girls, there is one outstanding fact. Irishwomen and girls, down to the very little ones, always wore long skirts. In most cases the skirts reached the ankles or brushed the shoes. At times young girls wore slightly shorter skirts, to the middle of the shin. But never shorter. The kilt, as well as not being Irish, is completely out of keeping with womanly grace and dignity, and can, when worn with black stockings and a vest covered with jingling medals, be very ugly and grotesque. However, these 'Irish kilts' and so-called 'Celtic costumes', invented in the uncritical enthusiasm of the early days of the National movement are now gradually being put away, and there is hope that genuine and handsome forms of Irish dress will replace them as national or local costumes of which we may be proud.

Plough and Spade

It is a very long time now since the cultivation of crops first began in this country, perhaps as long as five thousand years ago, perhaps only about four thousand – no one can say definitely. One thing, however, is certain, that the country in which our remote ancestors first began to till the soil was, in its wild and natural state, entirely unsuitable for any kind of tillage without laborious clearing and preparation. The greater part of the country was covered with woodland, some of it with forests of fine oak and other native timber, but with wide stretches under hazel, holly, thorn, briars and all sorts of scrubby thickets. Where there was no woodland there was heather or rock, bog or marsh, all untouched by the hand of man and all needing much care and labour to produce even the roughest kind of tillage land. Even today we can see proof of this, for if any field is left untilled and ungrazed it begins immediately to revert to the wild state; first come weeds, then briars, then bushes, and in ten years it is a jungle. Our ancestors had to begin with a jungle that had flourished unhindered for ages; they had to tame this wilderness and then keep it tame. Since so much wood and thicket had to be cleared we can imagine that their first weapons against the wild were fire and the axe – the trees and bushes were fired standing or else first hacked down and then burned – when, incidentally, the ashes helped to make the soil fertile. But once the ground was cleared of heavy growths the plough and the spade took over and have remained in the front line of the war against the wild, down to our own day.

Ireland rejoices in a mild, moist climate which promotes a luxuriant growth of grass, a growth which is almost entirely continuous from end to end of the year, not being entirely stopped by excessive cold in the winter nor killed by severe drought in the summer as it is in other parts of the world. This means that the soil of Ireland is covered by a strong sod of matted roots of grass and other surface vegetation, and the first and principal operation in tillage is the cutting, lifting and turning of this covering of sod. There are parts of the world, in the drier and warmer lands to the south, where such a covering of sod is not found, and where the surface of an untilled and unirrigated field in summer is mainly dust with sparse vegetation. Here the cutting and turning of a sod is not a necessary part of tillage, and the ground is worked by implements of the hoe or shovel type – as in many parts of Africa and southern Asia, or by light ploughs which have no mouldboard to turn a sod, but merely stir and break up the soil in the manner of our modern 'digger' plough.

How far back the plough goes in the history of Irish agriculture we cannot say. But it is quite clearly established as a normal implement in Early Christian times, say twelve hundred years ago. The iron parts of these ploughs, the coulters and shares, have been found in a number of places, and indicate that the type was a heavy wooden plough without a wheel. Then there is a lot of written evidence. The ancient Irish laws – the

'Brehon Laws' – have something to say about them. One
tract, which lays down the differences between the
various classes in the community, states that one of the
signs of a strong, independent farmer, is that he owns
a complete plough with all its gear. Another gives rules
for the smaller farmer who owns a plough in partner-
ship with his neighbours. The usual plough team was
four, or even six, oxen; although we know that horses
were also used, the ox or bullock was preferred for the
slow and heavy task of ploughing. There seem to be two
main reasons why the ox was preferred, first because the
horses known in Ireland at the time were small, light
animals, and second because the horse-collar which we
use now was unknown then, and the types of harness
that were used were unsuited for any heavy draught
work. In contrast to this the bullock was a strong, stout,
heavy beast, and when yoked by the head could exert
his weight and strength to the full. Just like the car and
the tractor nowadays, one very handy for light travelling
and the other well suited for slow heavy pulling.

An old type of plough appears to have continued in
use up to about two hundred years ago, although it
must be admitted that it was a very clumsy and in-
efficient implement by contrast with more recent
ploughs. Not one specimen of this plough is known to
have survived, but there are a few descriptions and a
number of drawings, none of which recommend its
revival even by the most ardent of Irish-Irelanders.
Some carvings on tombstones of the 17th and 18th
centuries show us that it had a wooden share-beam
resting on the ground, and above and parallel to this a
draught-beam which was secured to the share-beam

(the equivalent of the modern soleplate) by means of two upright wooden staves of which the rear one was prolonged upwards and backwards to form part of the handle. The coulter and soc were iron or steel, but the rest of the plough was wood. A team of from three to six horses was needed to pull one of these ploughs, and in most places the horses were harnessed abreast. In addition to the ploughman who held the handles and guided the plough, two other men were needed; one of them led the horses and the other walked beside the plough with a pole in his hand keeping the share in the soil by pressing on the beam. In some places a fourth man armed with a spade came on behind the plough turning the bits of sod which had escaped the pressure of the narrow straight mouldboard. There is evidence to show that, in backward places, horses were tackled to ploughs and harrows by the simple expedient of tying a trace to their tails, but this was forbidden by law and gradually died out. It is easy to see why the light, handy swing plough, whether made of wood or iron, rapidly took the place of the old clumsy type in the latter part of the eighteenth century.

Nowadays the spade is becoming more and more a horticultural implement only, very useful in the kitchen garden and the flower bed, but no more than an odd-job tool about the farm. But formerly, and not so long ago at that, it was a very important implement in Irish agriculture, for there were many of the more remote parts of the country where the use of the plough was almost unheard of and the fields were tilled exclusively with the spade, small fields of oats and potatoes in which both the corn and the root crop were planted in ridges,

a practice which has continued in a few places along
the west coast down to our own day. But there were
other areas, such as the fertile lands of Tipperary and
Kilkenny, where prosperous farmers found it more
economical, taking labour costs and crop return into
consideration, to till the big fields with the spade rather
than with the plough. Every year large numbers of
workmen from Kerry, Clare, Galway, Mayo, Leitrim
and Donegal made their way inland with their spades
on their shoulders to the 'hiring fairs' at which the
farmers made bargains with them for the spring and
autumn work. These were the migratory labourers, the
spailpíní fánacha who were such familiar figures in Ireland, and in England and Scotland too, in the eighteenth
and nineteenth centuries.

In many countries the spade is an implement for stirring and shifting earth, a descendant of the primitive
hoe. But in Ireland the spade is primarily an implement
for cutting and turning the sod, the essential first step in
almost any tillage operation in Ireland. The caracter-
istics of an Irish spade are a straight cutting edge, a
longish blade bent or cranked in the middle, a step by
the use of which the spade can be pushed into the ground
by the spadesman's foot and a long handle. But within
these limits there is a most astonishing variety in Irish
spades. Certainly no two counties use the same form of
spade, and often the shape changes from barony to
barony or even from parish to parish, so much so that a
spadesman from one district would find it very difficult
to use the spade of another district, and in some cases
would scarcely recognise the other implement as a spade
at all. Around Abbeyfeale on the Kerry-Limerick

border the spade iron is twenty inches long, five and a half inches wide across the edge of the blade and two and a half inches wide across the 'waist' of the blade. A spade in south County Leitrim will be fifteen inches long, two and a half inches across the edge and three and a half inches wide near the socket. This means that the Abbeyfeale specimen expands like a narrow fish-tail towards the edge, while its counterpart from Mohill is narrower at the edge than at the top. Around Portlaoise the old type of spade is fifteen inches long and six inches wide all the way up until it is narrowed suddenly to form a socket. All these spades are 'one-sided', a wooden step for the user's foot is driven into the socket beside the handle, always on the right side, unless the user is a 'ciotóg'. The most formidable of all the one-sided spades is the Cavan 'loy', which now has almost passed out of use. 'Them fellas that's going now wouldn't carry a loy' said an old workman from County Cavan, for although the loy iron was rather small, as spades go, say fourteen inches long and three inches wide at the edge, the handle was a stout beam expanding to as much as five inches wide and five inches thick a short distance above the iron; this expansion formed a bulge on the back of the handle which gave very strong leverage, and when turning the sod the loy was scarcely lifted from the ground but used rather like a hand operated plough.

The one-sided spade still holds its own in the south and west of Ireland, but it has long disappeared in most parts of Ulster and is on its way out in most parts of Leinster. Its place is taken by varieties of the 'two-sided' spade, which has an iron step on each side of the handle and thus can be used 'right-handed' or 'left-handed' as

desired. But these 'two-sided' spades no more conform
to one pattern than the 'one-sided' form. A specimen
from Cavan is twenty inches long, five and a quarter
inches wide at the edge and four inches wide at the top,
a long expanding blade, while one from Sligo is fourteen
inches long, three and three quarter inches wide at the
edge and four and a half inches wide at the top, a light
narrowing blade. Another, from near Glenties in Donegal, is sixteen inches long, six inches wide at the edge and
five and a quarter inches wide at the top. All these are
the blade dimensions, the socket is not included. To one
not used to the spade, the differences of quarters of
inches may seem of no importance, but they are of great
importance to the spadesman, as are ounces of difference
in weight, and inches of difference in the length of the
handle. Most parts of Ireland favour the long handle in
both spade and shovel; the usual standard for the total
length of the tool being that it should stand as high as its
user's shoulder. A turf *slean*, on the other hand, should
only come to the user's waist belt. One area in Ireland,
however, the north-east corner, favours a short handle
in the spade, with a little crosspiece, like the bar of the
letter T.

In the old days the spades, like all the other iron tools
and fittings, were made by the local smiths. And local
custom as well as local soil conditions led to the different
spade types – nearly two hundred different patterns in
Ireland, if we count all the variations in size, shape,
weight, amount of bend, and type of step and handle.
In recent times the spades are made in mills and
foundries, but the local custom still demands the old
types, and the factories have to conform by producing

scores of different shapes and sizes. Here is one, at least, feature of rural life in which dull uniformity has not forced the old ways out.

The Flail

Back in the 1920's the threshing machine was looked upon as the very last word in modern farming methods, and the day of the threshing was a very big day in the life of the farm. The neighbours turned up in force to give a helping hand. Men piking down the sheaves from the sheaf stack, men cutting the tyings and feeding the thresher, men shifting the grain sacks and more men making the straw stack. The womenfolk busy about the feeding of such a big *meitheal*. The owner of the thresher moving about importantly, stoking the boiler, adjusting here and tinkering there; everybody was, of course, in his working clothes but the threshing machine man always managed to look quite different to all the others – you could tell at a glance who was in charge of operations, while the owner of the farm looked just the same as any of the other ten or twenty busy men in the haggard. The big black steam tractor with its shiny brass and its fascinating smell of engine, the puffs of steam and smoke and the great belt that flew endlessly round and round. And above all the hum and roar of the machinery, and every small boy with a secret resolve that when he grew up he, too, would be an engineer and run a threshing machine of his own. But times have a way of changing, and many a small boy who watched with wonder now sees the combine harvester, just another machine among many machines, making short work of his wheatfields with little fuss and less romance.

It is a very far cry from these modern methods back to the days when the Dublin parliament found it necessary to pass and act (10 and 11 Charles I, 1634, ch. 17) 'To Prevent the unprofitable Custom of Burning of Corne in the Straw' which laid down pains and penalties for the farmers who 'doe for a great part, instead of threshing, burn their corn in the straw, thereby consuming the straw, which might relieve their cattel in winter, and afford materials towards the covering or thatching their houses; and spoiling the corn, making it black, loathsome and filthy.' This method of separating the grain from the straw must have been a very ancient one, and in spite of the law and the progress of farming it continued in use in parts of Ireland, as well as in other parts of Europe, until quite recently; there are people yet alive who have seen it done, as an emergency measure when bread or porridge was needed and there was no ground meal in the house. Somebody went to the stack and pulled out a few sheaves of oats or barley, laid them on the flag of the hearth and set fire to them. The ashes were then winnowed to come at the grain and the grain was rubbed clean, ground in the quern and there it was ready for use, with the added advantage that the heat had dried the grain and made the meal crisp and nutty. Of course this method could be applied only to a small quantity of grain at the time; its use was out of the question for a large corn harvest, especially where the farmer intended to market his crop. But it must have been fairly common, at least in parts of the country, if a law for its suppression was found to be necessary. And it appears that the law was applied at least fairly strictly. We read of the Sherrif of County Galway riding

out with his men in harvest time to enforce it – this was
in the 1690's – and coming to seek his supper in a house
where no bread was ready. The quick-witted housewife
laid before him a dish which held one sheaf of oats, and
when he asked the meaning of this curious meal she
answered that his own law prevented her from offering
him a proper cake. Whereupon the Sherrif allowed his
zeal to relax at least until his hunger was appeased, and
went out to look about the farm while the womenfolk
proceeded to make his supper in the time-honoured way.

Quite the opposite was done when good straw was
needed for thatching. Unskilful threshing might damage
the straw, and a thatcher with pride in his craft would
take no chances with bad material, and so the straw
must be 'lashed' to remove the grain. The worker took
the sheaf by the butt end and beat its head against
some hard object placed at proper height – it could be a
stone laid on a stool, or the edge of a barrel or the rungs
of a ladder. This was slow work but the straw was
uninjured. It also ensured that the grain was not
crushed, and some farmers used this method to produce
the seed for next year's crop; we are told that a good
worker could moderate his strokes to ensure that only
the better, riper grains were dislodged, while any un-
matured grains remained in the straw to be threshed
out later with the flail or fed unthreshed to the cattle.
And still another reason is given by Mr Dubourdieu in
the *Statistical Survey of County Antrim* which he wrote for
the Royal Dublin Society in the year 1812. With reference to wheat he says: 'Threshing is not approved of
unless the grain is very dry; when this is not the case it is
bruised on the barn floor (by the flails) and grows blue

moulded. Lashing is much better though mere tedious.'
And again he says: 'When wheat has smut, it is re-
commended to lash it, not to thresh it; for in lashing
the smut balls come out whole, and may, if not broken
by the feet, be easily separated from the sound grain
without injuring its colour.'

Another method, used for the same purposes, was
called 'scutching' or *scothbhualadh*. The worker took each
sheaf and beat the ear end gently with a short stick,
which dislodged the grain without injuring it or the
straw. Here again the skilled man could strike just hard
enough to knock out the riper grains for seed.

However, up to the coming of the threshing machine,
the principal and best known method was threshing with
the flail. Many Irish farmers of to-day have never seen a
flail in their lives, although their fathers would remember it well and it was an important item in their
grandfathers' stock of tools. Some men were famous for
the skilful use of this implement, like Kickham's Matt
the Thresher, and worked all through the harvest and on
into the winter and even the spring threshing for farmer
after farmer. A good thresher needed a good flail and
the thresher's motto was 'Colpán coill agus buailteán
cuilinn, laíthreán teann agus buille in aghaidh an phu-
nainn', 'A hazel handstaff and a holly striker, a springy
floor and a blow against the sheaf'. Great care was taken
in selecting the two sticks which made up the flail, in
their shaping and seasoning and in the way in which
they were hinged together. The floor, too, was an object
of care. Some farmers, especially in Leinster, threshed in
the barn on a clay floor which had been laid – gener-
ations earlier, perhaps – very carefully. There is a

tradition that a horse's skull buried under the floor made it very 'lively' and helped to produce a fine, brisk sound when struck by the flail; this was done in other countries, too, in Sweden, for instance, and because of the importance attached to the sound of the flails some Swedish farmers who threshed on a wooden floor stretched a steel wire on the under surface of the floor to increase the resonance. Some Irish farmers used wooden threshing boards, about six feet square; these were common in west Cork. But there were careless farmers who did not bother to prepare a floor – any old place, even the public road, would do.

Two rows of sheaves were laid on the floor, one on each side, heads inward so that the grain overlapped. The two threshers stood one on each side and struck alternate blows quickly and lightly in perfect timing and rhythm. When three men threshed together the timing was most expert, and woe betide the foolish man who fancied himself as a thresher and upset the work of his betters by mistiming a stroke. On a big farm several pairs might work together. The good thresher could turn the sheaf over with the butt of the handstaff or his boot toe without interrupting the rhythm of the work, and cast loose the binding of the sheaf with a quick thrust of the flail so as to come at the last of the grain. As soon as the two rows of sheaves were fully threshed the straw was taken away, the grain swept up and laid aside and another layer of sheaves arranged on the floor, all neatly and quickly. Some farmers kept strong linen sheets which were laid on the floor under the sheaves; these kept the grain clean and made its removal from the floor very simple. The threshers did not encourage onlookers, for who could tell when some silly person might come too near and get a good blow of the flail? Indeed the Ancient Irish Laws made it clear that a person struck by a flail could claim no compensation unless he could show quite clearly that he had some definite business on the threshing floor.

Four different ways of tying the flail were used in Ireland. In parts of the north a hole was bored through the top of the handstaff and the tying was passed through the hole and bound to the end of the striker; this was not the best form of tying as neither of the sticks could rotate in the tying, which made threshing more tiring as it put extra strain on the users hands. In other parts of the north and in many areas down the west the tying was bound to the striker but was looped around a groove in the handstaff, so that the striker could be made to revolve when swung. In another widely used method known in most of Munster and much of Connaught and Ulster the tying was a double loop resting in two grooves, one at the end of each of the sticks. But the most complicated, and probably the most efficient, tying was that used in Leinster and in some of the adjacent areas of the other provinces. Each of the sticks was fitted with a leather cap made by doubling a strong piece of hide over the end of the stick; the cap on the striker was firmly bound but that on the handstaff was cleverly secured on grooves so that the handstaff could twist around inside it. The two caps were then fastened together by a 'middle band' of leather. The tying of a flail was regarded as an expert's job, and different materials were fancied by different threshers. Sheepskin was commonly used, but the skin of a large eel was said to be the best of all for the job. Some favoured green horse- or cowhide, others swore by goatskin or even badgerskin. Flax tow had its devotees, and some skilful men plaited their tyings from slender willow twigs. And of course each district had its own name for the various parts. The Leinsterman's 'handstaff' was 'colapa' in Munster, 'colapán' in Connaught and 'láfrann' in Donegal. The Munsterman's 'buailteán' was 'buailtín' in Donegal and 'bóilcín' to the Cavanman, while most of the north called it a 'soople'. You had 'iall', 'gad', 'fong', 'hanging' and 'tug' in different areas for the tying.

The flail was very widely used in former times. It was in nearly every part of Europe and many parts of Asia. As far away as China it is still used to thresh both wheat and rice, but the Chinese are not content with one striker, they use at least two and some of their flails have as many as six. In the northern parts of Africa and parts of Asia, as well as in some areas of the south of Europe an entirely different method is still in use; the sheaves are spread on a large threshing floor and horses or oxen pull a form of roller over them, which is the origin of the proverb, 'Thou shalt not muzzle the ox that treadeth the corn'. In the old days in Ireland, too, the thresher was not muzzled, for it was dry and dusty work and cooling drinks were much in demand. And diet faddists should take note that the thresher's favourite refreshment was well-cooled fresh buttermilk.

The Dairy

Times change. Nowadays we look upon the stealing of cattle as a most reprehensible business, and on the rare occasions when it does happen, we have very little sympathy for the robbers when they are overtaken by the Law. But in the 'good old days' in Ireland it had all the appearance of an organised sport. Our ancient historical records are full of accounts of cattle raiding carried on by kings and princes and other important me1, and we can be sure that the ordinary man did not harg back when there was an opportunity of a profitable visit to his neighbour's byre or bawn. There was even a special class of literature describing this activity. The ancient epic describing the heroic deeds of Cuchulain and the warriors of the Red Branch is framed in a cattle raid, the Táin Bó Chuailgne, and there are several other spirited accounts of adventurous cattle raids in old Irish literature, so that the Cattle Raid was the ancient equivalent of the Detective Story of to-day. A Poet, to be recognised as fully qualified in his art, had to be able to recite a number of them and we can imagine that the lords and ladies sat enthralled and the lesser people crowded in to hear a visiting poet recite the tale of a Bigger and Better Cattle Raid Carried Out in Thomond. The successful raider was lauded to the skies, and it became more or less obligatory on the newly elected king or chieftain to show his skill and courage by carrying out a raid against some powerful neighbour. Another and, to us, even stranger custom was that the local monastery was entitled to a cow or a bullock from the spoils.

On the other hand, nobody carried out raids on the grand style to steal corn or other produce, and anybody who did commit such a theft was regarded as a plain thief, not as a romantic hero. In fact it is clear that the herdsman looked on himself as superior to the plowman, and the cattle breeder, the owner of the large herds was apt to look down on the husbandman whose back was bent over the spade. We know that the growing of corn always had an important place in Irish rural economy, but the place of cattle was greater still. We know that the human population of Ireland, say four hundred years ago, was considerably less than it is now, but the number of cattle in the country then appears to have been larger then than now. Cattle, and especially cows, are mentioned in thousands. In the year 1562 a report reached Queen Elizabeth that Shane O'Neill the Proud had just got away with ten thousand head of cattle from the territory of the O'Donnells, that is, Donegal. Eleven years later Turlough O'Neill improved on this by lifting thirty thousand head from his kinsman the Baron of Dungannon. Still another eleven years later the English forces, under the Lord President Norrys, raised the record by depriving Sorley Mac Donnell of over forty thousand head. And a careful estimate made by the English authorities reported that Hugh O'Neill, Earl of Tyrone, then fighting against the Queen, had at his disposal nearly half a million cattle of various kinds, including a hundred and twenty thousand milking cows. It is no wonder that we still reckon a man's wealth by the number of his cattle, and use 'the grass of a cow' as a handy measure of land.

With such multitudes of cattle we can expect that cattle products were an important part of the people's diet. There was meat in plenty, great joints roasting and huge cauldrons in which a whole yearling could be boiled at one time. Plates of meat and bowls of broth and marrowbones for everyone, even for the beggars who came to the door. But equally or even more important were the products of the dairy, for a very great part of rural economy, as far back as we can trace it, was based upon milk. It may be that cows, in ancient times, gave less milk than we would expect from our well fed animals, but there were so many cows and so much pasture that Ireland was really a land flowing with milk. An officer in the army of King James wrote from County Limerick in the year 1690 that the people there were 'the greatest lovers of milk I ever saw, which they eat and drink above twenty several sorts of ways, and what is strangest, for the most part love it best when sourest.' Of course the south-west was especially famous for its dairy herds. We read in the old tale of the Vision of Mac Con Glinne that the hero, a poet, was at his studies in Roscommon when he became hungry for 'whitemeats', that is, milk foods, and set out for Munster, because he knew that they were there in plenty. Later, when telling of his wonderful vision of the Land of Food, he speaks of a Lake of Milk, a Cape of Curds and a Mountain of Butter. He was offered a little drink 'as much as twenty men will drink' of 'yellow bubbling milk, the swallowing of which needs chewing, of milk that sounds like the snoring bleat of a ram as it rushes down the throat', and

saw many monster shapes of butter, curds, cheese and
cream as well as joints of meat, flitches of bacon, black
puddings and other rustic delicacies. Some accounts
give the impression that many people lived, at least
during the summer, almost entirely on milk products.

Butter, in the past as now, had an especially important
place, and the churning of butter must go back, in Ireland, for thousands of years. The dash churn may be the
oldest type; it is mentioned in the 'Brehon Laws' of over
a thousand years ago, and is still to be seen in use in a
few places. Fifty years ago it was used in many parts of
Ireland. There is another very old method of butter-
making which seems to have been used too, but was
never common here, in which the churn or milk container was hung from the roof and swung about or
shaken. An English visitor to west Connaught in 1699
was somewhat taken aback by the offhand way in which
butter was made in a small house in which he spent the
night, where the woman of the house 'claps in her right
almost up to the arm pitt, which she made use of instead
of a churn staff', a proceeding which, he says, 'made my
gutts wamble'. When he asked for a drink of water 'the
woman of the house tooke a square wooden vessell called
a meddar, all of one piece cutt out of a tree, and putting
some soure milke in it she carryed it to a cow for they
were all before their doores and with the milk made me
a syllibub, which they call troander. I was surprized at
the pleasing taste and extraordinary coldness of it, on
such a sudden.' He has many other things to say about
milk. He asked how they strained it. 'To satisfye me the
engine was brought to us, which was a round thing
made of the bark of a birch tree, of a conical figure, and

stuffed with cleane straw or grass, and through this they let theire milke run, by which the haires and dirt are seperated from it.' When they cooked a hare for supper they boiled it in a pot of melted butter – a form of cookery slightly on the expensive side nowadays. For breakfast they had another milk dish – 'The next morning a greate pott full of new milk was sett over the fire, and when it was hott they pour'd into it a pale full of butter milk, which made a mighty dish of tough curds in the middle of which they placed a pound weight of butter.' And this was in a poor and remote part of the country.

Usually the milk was set in large earthenware pans, and when the cream had risen it was skimmed off and put in large crocks until churning day, by which time the cream had become a bit sour, which gave 'country butter' its distinctive taste. But in some places all the milk, or most of it, was put into the churn with the cream and churned. Most farmhouses used the dash churn, and a big dash churn could be very tiring in use. Of course nobody should leave the house without taking a turn at it, this was said to be for good luck and to prevent the butter being 'taken', but it is likely that whoever began the custom was hoping for help in a very heavy job. Many dairies had a sort of spring arrangement for lifting the churn dash after it had been thrust down, which lessened the work greatly and enabled larger churns to be used. But the big farms used a 'barrel-churn', a large barrel with a pivot projecting from the centre of each end, so that it could be rotated on its axis by means of a crank handle – of course it was mounted on a strong stand. Vanes or flanges set inside

the barrel threw the milk about so that it was churned,
and this machine had a much greater capacity than a
dash-churn. Still larger churns worked by a horse, or
even a pair of horses, were used on the biggest farms.
In the latter half of the last century two types of churn
which were new to the Irish countryside came into use,
the small churn in which a wooden frame was revolved
by turning a crank, and the 'tumbling churn', a barrel
in which the pivots were fastened in the sides, so that it
turned end over end when the crank handle was worked.
In most parts of the country there was a good surplus of
butter over the family's own needs and this was sold.
There were big farmers who made a business of selling
butter and poor families that stinted themselves in order
to make up a firkin for the market. Most of the butter
sold in the market was exported, and Cork was the
centre of the butter export trade, handling three
hundred thousand firkins or more in the year a century
or so ago. And this great trade gave occupation not only
to the farmer and the butter merchant, but also to the
cooper who made the churns and firkins, the turner who
produced the piggins and skimmers, the carters who
carried the butter, the potter who made the milk pans
and cream-crocks and many others. Curiously enough,
there was very little making of hard cheese; many forms
of sour milk, curds and soft cheese were eaten, but for
whatever may be the reason, hard cheese was more or
less unknown. We all have heard the story of the girl
who was offered a slice of cheese when she visited the
town. Quoth she 'Má's cailín ó'n dtuath mé ní iosfainn
geir!' – 'I may be a country girl, but I do not eat
tallow!' Many older people in the Irish countryside will

remember the first time they saw cheese.

Butter making gave sour milk in many varieties.
There was the 'thick milk' left behind in the pans when
the cream was skimmed off, and the buttermilk left in
the churn when the butter was taken out. Both of these
were delicious drinks on a hot day. But fresh milk was
deliberately soured, too, by adding rennet or by setting
in a vessel with a trace of sour milk in it, as a drink or to
produce curds and whey. The whey was drunk and the
curds eaten in various forms. Sour cream was used, too,
as a dressing on mashed potatoes and other cooked vegetables, or on a salad called 'cabáiste Scotch' made of
white cabbage hearts and onions chopped together.

And think of the astonishing variety of beliefs and
customs that grew up around the dairy and the cow-
shed, all the ways of protecting the cattle and saving the
butter, all the things that were done at the milking and
churning, and on Saint Brighid's Eve and May Eve and
November Eve. And all the tales of witches becoming
hares and hags milking the spancel. Cattle have always
been on the Irish scene, and though we may go all out
for modern methods, the cow is still the cow and our
best friend. Well might the old Irish proverb say that
the stream of milk from the cow's udder is one of the
three threads that support the world.

Carrying Things

In modern times the carrying of things from one place to another is more important that ever it was before. It has become a major industry, employing thousands of people and directed by complicated organisations. It uses great numbers of machines, many of them of huge size, cars, lorries, trains, ships and aeroplanes. Most of the great discoveries and inventions and developments of recent times have been applied to the faster or safer or cheaper means of moving people or things from one place to another. And there is no slackening of effort in this field. Every day we hear or read of better cars, faster planes or bigger ships.

And yet there are parts of the world, although now they are few and far between, where primitive people have no other method of transport than carrying things on their backs or in their arms. You have to go to the wilder parts of Australia or the jungles of the Amazon to find this now, but a couple of hundred years ago there were many parts of Africa, America and Asia where it was the common method. Sometimes it still must be done for special reasons, for a man can carry a load over rough country where no animal can travel. A few years ago, when Everest, the highest mountain in the world, was climbed, all the material and apparatus needed was carried many miles by porters specially accustomed to this work.

Of course people will carry things as long as the

human race exists. The day when handbags and umbrellas are completely self-propelled may never dawn. Women will continue to carry shopping bags and tennis rackets and men will still shoulder shovels and oars and guns. But the sight of men and women as beasts of burden is passing away. People carried heavy loads long distances because there were no roads or cart tracks, or because they did not know of any other way, or – most often – because they were too poor to use other methods. In many countries, our own among them, these reasons have almost entirely disappeared, and with them the necessity of straining under loads.

Is there any part of Ireland where women still carry things on their heads? A century ago it was a common sight; fifty years ago it was still common, and in some places it was done until quite recently. Many of us remember seeing countrywomen carrying buckets of water or cans of milk on their heads, and many old countrywomen still alive owe their stately carriage to their youthful skill in carrying things balanced on their heads. When we see some elderly woman going the road with the walk of a queen, we may feel some regret that her daughters and her granddaughters have given up the old custom. Quite heavy loads can be carried in this way. In Ireland men hardly ever practised this, but there are other countries where men commonly do it. A photograph published some years ago showed six stalwart men in the street of a town in Brazil marching along with a piano on their heads.

Men, on the other hand, often carried heavy loads on their shoulders, while women did not. No special apparatus was required; you just heaved the sack or beam or whatever it was on to your shoulder and walked away. At most you put a pad under the weight to soften a rough surface or a sharp edge. Shoulder yokes were used in Ireland, but only in a few places, for carrying a pair of buckets. These yokes were made of wood, fitted to the shoulders and with a projection on each side from which the buckets hung, so that the hands were free to steady the yoke or the buckets when necessary. They were much more used in England and in parts of the Continent, while in China, for instance, they were used very commonly for carrying all sorts of loads.

But people always knew that the best way to carry a load is to secure it on the broad of the back, and many forms of ropes, nets, frames, baskets and bags have been developed for the purpose. The hiker's rucksack and the soldier's pack can hold an astonishing amount of kit and equipment and can be carried day after day without undue fatigue. But the feats performed in the past in carrying loads in back-baskets leave the hikers and the soldiers far behind. What about the fisherman from Teelin who landed his catch of salmon at the foot of Slieve League, packed it – nearly a hundredweight – into a back basket, put it on his back and climbed the crazy path up the thousand foot cliff and then walked the twenty-five miles into Mountcharles to sell it? Many a field was manured by women carrying seaweed or sand or manure, in baskets on their backs, and many a road was made in the bad times from stones and gravel carried in the same way by gangs of women while the men quarried and broke the stones and laid the road. People carried fish and potatoes and even small live animals to market in back-baskets and pedlars used them to carry their wares. Light bulky stuff, like hay or wool, was tied in a bundle and slung on the back; there were special nets or ropes for this, and there were wooden frames for carrying stuff already in sacks, boxes or casks.

When men began to use animals to carry loads they first put the burden on the animal's back. Occasionally we still see a pony or a donkey being led along with a sack of flour or grain balanced on its back, but bigger loads can be carried more safely by some form of pack-saddle. The commonest form in Ireland was the *srathar fhada*, a kind of straddle from which a large basket or pannier hung on each side. Formerly they were very common and were used to bring loads of all sorts to market, but their use on horses has almost entirely died out, and they are found on donkeys only in bringing turf out of bogs. They are becoming rarer and rarer and many people have never seen one in use. Which recalls the story of the Dublin man in Kerry. Said the Dublin man 'Excuse me, can I take a photo of your donkey with the baskets, for I never saw the like before?' Replied the Kerryman 'You never saw one before? Oh man, you must be from a very backward part of the country!'

Probably the oldest form of vehicle is a branch cut from a tree. It is not easy to drag a load over rough ground, and even on smooth ground the load may suffer. But a good leafy branch can be piled with fire-wood or hay or the carcass of a deer and hauled along by the stem. Once that step was thought out it required only a little imagination to produce a rudimentary sledge, and many sledges still have the triangular form of the tree branch. But the simple sledge on two runners is the commonest form. Usually we think of the sledge in connection with the colder parts of the world, with journeys over ice and snow, but sledges are very widely used for transport over rough or boggy ground. Those whose knowledge of Ireland comes from travelling along the roads may be surprised to learn that sledges, or 'slipes' as they are usually called, are still in common use in the country. There is hardly a county in Ireland in which they are not to be found. Within ten miles of the centre of Dublin they are used in hauling rocks out of the hill fields. Farther on in County Wicklow they are fitted with a 'rail' and haul turf from the bog to the roadside. And so on all through the country, from Kerry to Antrim and from Mayo to Wexford, for moving rocks on hill slopes and for bringing out the turf. They are usually small in size, four or five feet long and about three feet wide. Those used for hauling stones are smaller and more strongly made and often have a shallow 'box' of strong planks. Lighter and larger ones are used for turf and many of these have a 'rail' or 'creel' which in some cases is permanently secured and in others can be taken off when necessary. Another application of the sledge principle is the 'plough slipe'; this is a sort of runner of wood or iron, about a yard long and fitted with hooks or loops which hold the sock of the plough so that the runner lies under the sole-plate. By this means the plough can be pulled over the fields or along the road, guided in the ordinary way, without injury either to the plough or the surface over which it is pulled. But this appliance was never very common in Ireland.

Another type of wheelless vehicle, quite different

from the sledge or slipe, is the 'slide-car', still used in a few parts of Ireland and in many places abroad. If you take the wheels off an ordinary 'common cart' and get the horse to pull it along sliding on the back shafts you have a 'slide-car'. The real slide-cars were lighter and smaller than the common horse's cart and naturally did not have any axle or axle-beam, but the horse was harnessed between the shafts in the usual way and the back-shafts were fitted with strong wooden shoes to take the wear and tear; a new pair of shoes could easily be put on when the old ones were worn out. They were very useful on rough ground, for the slide bumped over holes, ruts and small rocks which would stop a wheel. Another advantage on hill slopes was self-braking. The heavier the load the more the drag and the less danger of the cart overrunning the horse; this braking effect could be increased by the driver stepping up on the slides and pressing them against the ground. These slide-cars continued in use up to our own time in a few places as far apart as Tory Island in County Donegal and Clear Island in County Cork, but the only district where they are at all common nowadays is around Glenhull in County Tyrone.

We know that fine chariots with light bodies and well-made spoked wheels were used in ancient times in Ireland. We read of chariots used by Cuchulain, by Saint Patrick and Saint Brighid and by many kings, ecclesiastics and warriors, both for peaceful travelling and for fighting. There are carvings of these chariots on some of the high crosses which are about a thousand years old, so we can see that they were two-wheeled vehicles, some with two shafts for a single horse and

others with a pole for two horses. They were light and
fast and could be driven at a gallop over suitable ground.
But these were costly vehicles, valued at the equivalent
of twelve good milking cows or so – the equivalent of a
motor-car in our own times. Some cost even more; we
read of one specimen which was worth eighty-four cows,
that is well up to Rolls-Royce standard. So the ordinary
man had to be content with a more humble type of
vehicle, and the farmers' carts mentioned in the ancient
laws must have been the direct ancestors of the solid-
wheeled carts in use all over Ireland up to a hundred
years or so ago, the famous 'low-backed car' on which
the poet met Sweet Peggy upon a market day. In these
carts the wheels were solid and were mounted on a
heavy wooden axle in such a way that the axle turned
with the wheels. The wheels were small in diameter,
only about two feet across, so that the shafts sloped backwards when the cart was harnessed to a horse. In some
cases the back end of the floor was raised on a beam
supported by uprights, so that the floor was level when
the cart was in use, but in others there was only a rail
at the rear end and the floor sloped backwards. But on
these carts loose loads, such as turf or potatoes, were
usually carried in a large 'kish' or basket woven of stout
hazel or sally rods and made to fit tightly into the cart,
so that the slope of the floor was not important, and might
be of some advantage in throwing most of the weight
back and thus lightening the pressure on the horse's
back. The axle was up to six inches in diameter and, as
we have seen, turned with the wheels. It was secured to a
pair of bolsters on the undersides of the shafts by two
semicircular hoops of iron in which it freely revolved.

But when the cart was in motion the weight of the shafts pressed upon the axle and liberal greasing was needed to overcome the friction. But this provided a form of self-braking, like that of the slide-car, and the greater the load the more the braking, which was a decided advantage when coming down a slope although a drawback when travelling on the level. The fixed wheels made turning more difficult, as the either inner wheel or the outer tore over the ground on the turn, with wear on both the wheel and the ground surface.

These low-backed cars were common in town and country a century ago, but the coming of the 'Scotch cart', the more efficient common cart of to-day, brought their use to an end in most places. Now they are to be found only in North Country Antrim and in South County Tipperary, and their days are numbered in these last refuges, for every year sees fewer and fewer of them in use.

In England and in many parts of the Continent the four-wheeled waggon is the common working vehicle on the farms. But the waggon never came into use in Ireland, where the one-horse cart always has been the working vehicle. Ireland shares this type of vehicle with Scotland and Norway to the north, while to the south the use of the two-wheeled cart stretches through southern France, Spain, Italy and the whole Mediterranean region, and so across Asia to India and China. The waggon, on the other hand, belongs to England, Holland, Denmark, Germany, Central Europe and Russia.

The coming of the tractor and the lorry has dealt a heavy blow to horse drawn transport. Carts are still

used on the farm, but get fewer and fewer on the roads.
And the old forms, the slipes and slide-cars and low-
backed cars are, except for a few survivors, gone. And
meanwhile the motor-car has made an even cleaner
sweep of the passenger vehicles, the traps and side-cars,
the back-to-backs and dogcarts, the noddies and jingles,
the cabs and coaches, the waggonettes and Bianconi
long cars. Travel to-day may be faster and more comfortable, but it is no safer or surer. And as to appearance,
what car can equal a high stepping horse?

Travel by Water

It is very quiet along the river now. The wind rustles the reeds and the swallows dip and wheel over the water. Sometimes an angler's boat chugs along on its outboard engine. Sometimes half a dozen schoolboys in a rowing-boat bring a moment of sound and movement. And sometimes, on a summer evening, an old man comes to sit on a stone bollard on the little grass-grown quay, to smoke his pipe and think back to the days when the river was a highway of traffic and when he himself was a small boy on this very quay revelling in the life and bustle of it all, the tarry smell of the boats, the coiled ropes, the carts piled high with sacks of grain, swinging derricks, trampling horses, farmers' boys shouting, bargemen cursing. And himself right there in the middle of it. Ah! those were the days!

Roads were none too good in the old days, and carts and waggons were slow. It was very much more convenient to send your goods by water if there was a suitable waterway, and it was not until the spread of the railways that carriage and travel by water began to fall off. The coming of motor traffic and transport, within the present century, has finished it.

In very ancient times, when the country was heavily wooded and there were no roads of any kind, the big rivers were the main travel routes. Our early ancestors were experts at making boats by hollowing out tree trunks, a practice which continued down to a couple of hundred years ago, when these boats were generally used and known as 'cotts'. Hundreds of them have been found in the rivers and lakes during drainage works, some of them up to forty feet in length. Indeed, it was the disappearance of the woodlands in the seventeenth and eighteenth centuries that stopped the making of these useful boats: as long as there were suitable trees they were made and used. Of course there were other kinds of boats, too, from little skiffs to barges which carried many tons of goods. There was hardly a river or a lake which did not have its own pattern of boat, and there were hundreds of skilled boatmen on the rivers and lakes, not to speak of the thousands of seafarers and fishermen along the coast. People lived close to the water in more ways than one; they were conscious of the sea, the rivers and the canals just as we are conscious of the roads and the airports, and when they had to travel or to convey merchandise, they first considered the possibility of doing it by water. This was especially the case in time of war or disturbance, when the side that could control the coast and the waterways had a great advantage in easy, though slow, communication. In 1600, Carew the President of Munster was short of stores during his expedition to Kerry and was glad to hear 'that the victuals which he expected from Corke were arrived at Carrighowlough in Thomond (i.e. Carrigaholt), almost opposite to the River of Cassan in Kerry, from whence in Boats they were transported up the Cassan to Lixnaw, foure miles into the Countrey, which service was performed by the ayde of the Earle of Thomond's boats.' Who would think, nowadays, of sending goods from Cork to Lixnaw by boat?

So important were the waterways that steps were
taken to construct new ones – the canals. This work was
begun on a large scale a little over two hundred years
ago, the object being to connect the Shannon and the
Barrow-Nore-Suir with Dublin, and to link the system
by branch canals to other centres. The work was very
heavy in the days before the motor-lorry and the steam-
shovel. Large gangs of workmen worked with pick and
shovel, and long lines of carts shifted the clay and stone.
Our word 'navvy', meaning a labourer engaged in heavy
work, comes from this; many of the canal companies in
Britain and Ireland were called 'Inland Navigation
Companies', so that the workmen were dubbed 'navi-
gators', or 'navvies' for short. The making of the main
Irish canals began about 1750 and went on for nearly a
hundred years, and the sytem was at its best and most
extensive just about the time of the coming of the canal's
first great rival, the railway. In 1840 goods could be sent
by safe inland routes from Limerick to Mullingar, or
from Clonmel to Ballinasloe, or from Kilkenny to
Longford. Hundreds of barges were in use carrying all
sorts of goods; the produce of the countryside, the butter,
grain, malt, potatoes to the towns, and the manufactured
goods of the towns to the countryside. Barges piled high
with barrels and boxes passed barges laden with turf,
coal or lime. Horses pulled the barges along the canals
and some of the rivers; the horse (usually one to each
barge) walking along a towpath beside the water. Many
of the barges were owned by the canal or transport
companies, but others were private and sometimes the
bargeman and his wife and family lived in the barge.
Carriage by canal was not at a very cheap rate; we are

told that it cost 10/7½d. to have a ton of flour sent from Carlow to Dublin, and 7/- to bring a ton of coal from Dublin to Carlow. It is to be feared that the canals never really paid for themselves, for the cost of making them was very high; the Grand Canal and its branches cost an average of twelve thousand pounds per mile, or just on £2,000,000 for the full 160 miles. Only a very large volume of traffic could justify such expenditure, and, just as the future seemed bright, along came the railways and eclipsed the canals.

One very interesting aspect of canal traffic was the passenger service, which began in 1780. The passenger boats were about fifty feet long and ten feet wide, most of this space being taken up with a very large cabin which had accommodation for forty-five first class and thirty-five second class passengers. Like the ordinary barges, these boats were pulled by horses, and the speed was little over four miles an hour. The journey from Dublin to Shannon Harbour, near Banagher, took eighteen hours and cost one guinea, first class, and 14/- for second class. Dublin to Moneasterevan cost 5/- and Dublin to Millingar 12/6 first class. Because the journeys took so long it was necessary to provide refreshment for the travellers, and a very good catering service was established. The cabins ran the length of the boat and had glass sides, so that the passing scene might be observed. There were rows of comfortable, cushioned seats, under which foot-warmers were put in winter time. Between the seats were the tables on which the travellers dined, or played cards or wrote letters (packs of cards and writing materials were provided). The roof of the cabin was flat, fitted with seats and covered with an awning, and when the weather was fine the passengers sat here at their ease, the gentlemen smoking or taking snuff (smoking was forbidden in the cabin, to spare the ladies, and gambling was forbidden on sundays, to spare the conscience of the Canal directors). The passengers were not stinted at mealtime. 'We had an excellent dinner on board, consisting of a leg of boiled mutton, a turkey, ham, vegetables, porter and a pint of wine each at four shillings and tenpence a head' reported one traveller from Athy to Dublin in 1803. But nobody, according to the regulations, was allowed more than one pint of wine, those who wished for more were consoled with the information that they might top up on porter, beer or cider to their hearts' content. It must have been a very pleasant way of travelling, for the Canal Companies had built fine hotels at suitable places, where the passengers spent the night in comfort. One class-conscious Englishman remarked with satisfaction that careful distinction was made throughout between the first and second class passengers, 'the latter may not always be of the most decent order but due precaution is taken to prevent their giving offence to the first cabin'. This gentleman had paid 12/6 for his fare, as against 7/7 for the second class – talk about tuppence ha'peny not talking to tuppence!

With the improvement of the roads in the 1820's and 1830's the coaches made better time, and the canals tried to rival this with 'fly-boats', fast boats pulled by a team of three horses at the gallop, making up to ten miles an hour; but it was too late, the days of the canals were already coming to an end.

If you try to cross the Shannon now, say from Tarbert

to Kilrush, or from Kilteery to Cahircon you may have a
very long wait for a boat and a very long search for a
boatman, yet well within the memory of the middle-aged
there were steamboats plying up and down and across
the river. From Listowel to Kilkee was a pleasant half-
day's run on boat and bike for the young men and
women of our father's generation. To-day it is a car
journey of well over a hundred miles. Many people will
remember the paddle steamer *Mermaid* which plied between Limerick and Kilrush, calling at several piers on
the way, zigzagging across the river – a service which
carried up to twenty-four thousand passengers in one of
its good years. Another service ran from Killaloe to
Athlone, and this carried up to 15,000 passengers a year
in its heyday.

Traffic between points along the coast was equally
important and frequent. The number of vessels registered in the various ports a century or so ago comes as a
surprise to us. Many of them were very small boats
engaged in the coastal and river trade, but, not counting
fishing boats, there were in the year 1851, 444 vessels
registered at Dublin, 462 at Belfast, 409 at Cork and 101
at Limerick and so on down the list until we come to 28
at Dundalk, 27 at New Ross 11 at Coleraine and 5 at
Westport, hundreds upon hundreds of ships, large and
small plying along the coast, not to mention the ocean-
going ships from other countries, tall full-riggers, schoon-
ers from Arklow and Wexford, Dutch galliots, odd
looking craft from the Baltic and the Black Sea. Those
were the days, indeed, when we looked out across the
water and when small boys could find high adventure
on the busy quaysides.

Weighing and Measuring

Nowadays when a housewife goes into the grocer's shop and buys a pound of tea she can be reasonably certain of two things, that she really is getting tea and that it weighs a standard pound. It might cross her mind, too, that she could go into a grocer's in any part of Ireland, or for that matter, England or Scotland, and get exactly the same quantity of the same commodity in response to her request for a pound of tea. In the same way, if a farmer orders ten tons of ground limestone he knows he will get an exact standard measure; if a further burst of enthusiasm brings him to order a second ten-ton lot a week later he expects to get an exactly similar quantity and quality. And when, in due course, his beet is accepted at the sugar factory he knows that it will be weighed, measured and tested according to exact standards and that he and his fellow suppliers will be paid according to a fixed scale. Nothing is left to chance or guesswork, for the growing complexity of our modern life makes the knowledge and acceptance of a set of exact standards absolutely necessary.

But things were done very differently in former times.

We can well imagine what conditions of trade and commerce were like in Ireland five or six thousand years ago, when our remote ancestors had not yet mastered the art of farming and still lived mainly as gatherers of food, as hunters and fishermen and collectors of roots, berries, shellfish, eggs and so on.

Suppose a hunter has been lucky and has brought down three deer in one chase, much more than he needs for his own family. Faced with the problem of disposing of the surplus meat he thinks of a neighbour who is an expert at making stone arrowheads, and off he goes with a deer's carcase on his shoulder to make his bargain. Each side examines what the other has to offer and the bargaining depends very much on present circumstances. If the hunter is out of arrowheads and the neighbour has plenty of food in store, the deer may go for six, but if the neighbour's children are hungry the hunter can hold out for a much higher price, a dozen or even twenty arrowheads. Later when enterprising traders from the Mediterranean arrived on the coast, the local people hurried down with their products, and were very willing to swop their valuable furs for the glass beads and other wonderful things exhibited by the cunning merchants. This kind of exploitation of people who were not expert in the ways of the world went on until quite recently, especially in Africa and America. The traders came with glass beads, copper rings, mirrors, brightly coloured cotton, knives axes and nails, and bartered a few shillings' worth of these for a bale of furs or an elephant's tusk or a bag of gold dust worth many pounds.

It is not so long since barter died out in our own country, and there are still places where people occasionally swap their surplus products instead of taking them to the market. And there still are a few travelling traders who exchange useful articles for eggs and other farm produce, or give toys to children who bring them jam-jars or waste paper. Special circumstances gave rise to local variants of barter. In the old days of the sailing

ships the route from America to Derry, Belfast and
Glasgow passed close to Tory Island at the north west
corner of County Donegal, and when the Tory fishermen
saw a topsail lifting over the horizon they launched their
boats loaded with potatoes, fresh vegetables, fish, eggs,
fowl and milk – all fresh foods which the people on the
ship had not tasted for weeks, and bargained briskly for
rum, tobacco, ropes, tools and other necessary articles.
The coming of the fast steamships put an end to this
trade.

This kind of barter was all very well in its way, but
the need for some standard form of weighing and measuring became obvious at a very early stage of civilisation.
It is quite clear that the first rough standards of measurement were based on the human body. A merchant
might announce that he would sell his salt at so much a
handful and be able to calculate his profit quite accu-
rately since he had already counted the number of handfuls in his bags when he was filling them; thus he had
made a standard for himself, one which was easily
understood by everybody. We still use this system. All
our measures of length are based upon the standard
yard of three feet measured with scientific accuracy, but
the foot was, of course, the length of a man's foot and the
yard the length of his walking pace; we still commonly
use our own foot and our own pace as a rough measurement. In the Middle Ages if a dispute arose about
measurement a Sheriff or other official was empowered
to go to the church door on Saturday and take the first
twelve men who came out; these were put standing in a
line with the toe of each man's shoe touching the heel of
the man in front, so that the length of the twelve feet,

measured with care, gave a good average which was taken as a standard, and the dispute decided on it. Women still measure cloth in fingers and men reckon the height of horses in hands. The width of a man's thumb was taken as an inch, and the distance from fingertip to elbow as half a yard. When a sailor was measuring rope he stretched his arms out fully and the amount of rope from hand to hand was a fathom. We use expressions of this kind in our daily speech. 'Give the horse a handful of oats', 'Throw a *gabháil* of hay to the cow', 'Put a pinch of salt in it', Come on in for a mouthful of tea'. We talk of a 'bit of soap' or a 'sup of petrol' although very few of us would really like to measure soap by biting it or petrol by taking a mouthful of it. But the words mean just that.

Uniformity of standard came only gradually. Our word mile comes to us from the Romans and meant a thousand paces. But there are several different miles still in use; we still speak of 'Irish' miles as well as statute miles, and a mile on the sea is different from a mile on the land. And although the countries of Europe have nearly all adopted the Metric System, the 'mile' is still a traditional measure in many of them. The Italian mile is nearly the same as our statute mile, but the Dutch mile is several hundred yards shorter and the Danish mile is equal to four and a half statute miles. So, when abroad, stick to kilometres, as the answer to the question 'How many miles is it?' may be very misleading. The same confusion is found in many other measures. Here in Ireland, as in Britain, there were two different gallons in use up to 1824, the 'wine gallon' and the 'ale gallon', with a difference of about a pint and a half between them. In 1824 a new gallon, bigger than the 'wine gallon' and slightly smaller than the 'ale gallon' was made standard, and we still use it. But the old 'wine gallon' is still the legal standard in the United States of America.

There was even greater variation in many of the measures used in the country a hundred and fifty years ago. A barrel of potatoes was 20 stone in Monaghan, 21 stone in Navan, 25 stone in Kells and 32 stone in Armagh. In Country Clare the stone of potatoes was 16 lbs in summer and 18 lbs in winter. The hundredweight of coal was 112 lbs in Dublin, but the hundredweight of oatmeal or beef was 120 lbs. The stone of oats was 14 lbs, the stone of tallow was 15 lbs and the stone of feathers was 16 lbs, so that a stone of feathers was really heavier than a stone of corn. The situation was summed up very well by a man who visited County Meath – which seems to have revelled in local differences – and reported 'The great diversity of weights and measures used throughout this County, and the different quantities under the same denomination in different parts of it, are productive of infinite trouble and perplexity'. Even today a novice might be slightly perplexed by the differences in the barrels used in measuring wheat, oats and barley. It is just as well that the Sugar Company did not introduce some special measure such as 'One barrel of sugar beet = $21\frac{1}{2}$ stone', but such a measure would be every bit as logical as some of those we still use every day.

It is, of course, easy to see how confusion may arise in efforts to reconcile a system of weights with one of cubic measure. An old scale of measures gives these equivalents for County Dublin: 1 stone = 1 bushel of bran, $3\frac{1}{2}$ stone

= 1 bushel of oats, 4 stone = 1 bushel of barley, 5 stone = 1 bushel of wheat. But in other parts you could find 7 stone of oats = 1 skibbal (Clare), 11 stone of oats = 1 kilderkin and 3 kilderkins = 1 barrel of oats (Cork), 24 stone of oats = 1 sack (Sligo), 6 stone of oats = 1 measure. (Tyrone) Pity the poor grain merchant!

In measuring land our ancestors took more note of its productive value than of its area. We still reckon the size of a man's farm in terms of the number of cattle which it will support: it may appear as a farm of thirty five acres in official returns, but the neighbours refer to it as 'the grass of ten cows', for they know well that on poorer land not far away it would take sixty acres to feed the same number of cows. Under the old methods of farming this was quite sensible, but in our day when there are so many ways of improving land the 'grass of ten cows' farm may easily carry fifteen or more, which would greatly surprise the old great-grandfather if he were still alive. When it came to reckoning shares in common pasture the ancient unit was the 'collop', which is already mentioned in the Brehon Laws of over a thousand years ago, and is still remembered in most parts of Ireland although seldom used now; in parts of the north and west it is called a 'sum'. The collop or sum is the amount of pasture which will support a certain animal for the grazing season, and in most parts of Ireland the animal taken as the unit was a fully matured cow, say a four-year-old. The other animals were then equated to this unit. Three horses were equal to four collops, and one collop was equal to four sheep, six goats or eighteen geese. In some places the proportion was different. In County Donegal, where light horses were used in the old days, the collop was one horse or one cow. The grazing method of geese uprooted the grass instead of biting it through without damaging the root, and for that reason geese were discouraged on common pasture by reducing the number allowed to a collop. This variation was, however, of no great impor- ·tance, for the collop was a local standard which, in the case of each farmer, referred to a proportion of a certain specific area of common pasture in which he had grazing rights.

Entirely different methods were used to measure tillage land. Exact measurement was no problem for the farmer tilling his own fields, for he knew their size and their productivity, but it was very important in the letting of tillage land and was everybody's concern in a country like ours where there was – and in places still is – so much conacre, 'score ground', 'quarter ground', rundale and other ways of giving or taking land for tillage. The units of measurement usually referred to the method of tillage. A 'ploughland' or *seisreach* was origi- nally the amount of land which one team of oxen could plough in a season; later it became more or less standard- ised at 120 acres. Another unit of measurement was the 'spade', usually five and a half feet long, used in meas- uring land tilled with the spade, as almost all potato land and much corn land was in the last century. Local variations are known here, too, but again these are not important, as this was a purely local standard of meas- urement. In many places the standard portion of land which was let for tillage was the 'quarter of ground'; in County Limerick this was reckoned as 'eight hundred spades of *bán* four feet wide' or one quarter of a Plantation acre. But the word 'Quarter' or *ceathrú* also meant the quarter of a townland, which was a ploughland or 120 acres. Other land units were the 'gneeve', *gníomh*, reckoned at ten acres, the 'sessiagh' of twenty acres, and the *taite* of sixty acres. In places there were odd-sounding local units of land, such as 'gallons', 'noggins', 'ounces', 'pottles' and so on, and the stranger needed all his powers of observation to know what was meant by these terms. Indeed, humorous terms of measurement were used to describe certain forms of work. 'He measured that garden by feet' meant that he dug it all with the spade, and 'to measure it in handfuls' meant to reap corn with the hook (the reaper grasped the straw in his left hand while he cut it with his hook), and the saying was that these were the two most laborious ways of measuring land. In most places turf was reckoned by the *sleán*, which was as much as a good workman could cut in one day and gave about three tons of dry turf in good quality bog.

Ways of weighing and measuring are becoming more and more standardised. A trader no longer needs to bring his own scales and measures along with him, and since the custom of clipping little bits off the edges of coins has ceased it is no longer necessary to weigh the coins in business transactions. And it is no longer necessary for the merchant to examine each single item which passes through his stock, as he had to do in former times. The ancient laws of Ireland laid down that an inch was the length of three grains of wheat, and that a silver penny weighed the same as eight grains of wheat, while the basic unit of volume was the hen's egg. An elaborate and highly unworkable system of weights and measures was built up from these, so that it is, perhaps, just as well that in this respect we do not return to the ways of our ancestors, especially when we remember that the basic unit of value in ancient Ireland was the female slave.

The Water Diviner

In these distant days when a pump in the yard was close to the summit of the countryman's ambition in the matter of water supply I saw a water diviner searching for a well in our backyard. He was a local man, a farmer's son of about thirty years of age, one of the neighbours with nothing mysterious about him, a quiet, well spoken fellow that came of respectable people, not a bit different from any other countryman of his age, except that he could find water. All the countryside knew that, and accepted it as a fact, just as they accepted as a fact that one man had good eyesight and another keen hearing and a third the gift of healing a stye in the eye with his fasting spit.

While he passed the time of day with the older people we were examining his divining instrument with all the curiosity and keen observation of children. He called it a 'rod' but it was really a forked stick, a *gabhlóg* of smooth hazel, the stem about half an inch in diameter and a foot long, and each of the branches about eighteen inches long and not quite as thick as the stem. It was seasoned and supple, but no different from any hazel fork as we all knew; it was the instrument he worked with, just as one man worked with a spade, another with a saw or another with a crowbar.

Then he began. He settled the rod in a peculiar grip. One prong of the fork was clasped in each hand, and his hands were held palms upwards and thumbs outwards, so that the ends of the fork stuck out between his thumbs and forefingers, and the stem of the fork pointed forward, from him. His arms were stretched forward, as if he were pointing the fork at something level with himself in the distance. Holding it like this he walked slowly across the yard and we all saw the rod twitching upwards when he came to a certain point. He drew a line with his heel there and went over the ground the same way again and, as we expected, the rod acted in much the same way as the first time. Still he was not satisfied; he approached that part of the yard from several different directions, making numbers of marks on the ground with his heel according as the rod indicated. Then he looked thoughtfully at the ground for a while and finally gave his verdict. There was water, plenty of it. Twenty-seven feet deep the well must be. They must not mind any water coming in higher than this – the main supply was at twenty-seven feet. He could not say how pure the water was; there might be iron in it, there was in most of the water in the place. But it certainly was there, plenty of water. Nobody questioned his findings, and in a few days' time the tedious job of sinking a well in the old fashioned way began. And, weeks after, at twenty-seven or twenty-eight feet, there was the water, floods of it. And sure enough there was iron in it, not very much, but you'd notice it in the tea. The well is there yet, never once having run dry in forty years, although a force-pump fills a big tank from it now. He refused to take any fee for his work, saying that it was only a little thing to do for a neighbour, and that the compliment would be returned some time. To us children it seemed a very big thing indeed, especially as we had seen the sweat running down his face as he paced the yard with his rod.

Nobody knows how ancient this art may be, but there is no doubt that it is very old. The seventeenth-century historian Dr. Geoffrey Keating retells a story of the time of Cormac Mac Airt, when that doughty monarch marched against the King of Munster and besieged him in a stronghold close to the present Knocklong. The Munstermen began to suffer greatly from lack of water and their king, Fiachaidh Muilleathan, had to do something about it. As Keating recounts 'People and cattle were on the point of death through want of water, and the King of Munster was obliged to send for Mogh Ruith, a druid who was in Ciarraí Luachra. And when Mogh Ruith came, the King had to give him two stretches of land at Fermoy which are called Roche's Country and Condon's Country. And thereupon Mogh Ruith released water for the King of Munster's army, by throwing a magic dart into the air, and where the dart fell a well of pure water sprang out, and relieved the Munstermen from their thirst. And with that the King of Munster and his army fell upon Cormac and his men and drove them out of Munster, without their having won a victory or taken plunder.' Apparently water divining was included in the repertoire of all the best druids, and it was lucky for the King of Munster that he had one within calling distance, even if it did cost him a couple of thousand acres of land as good as any in County Cork.

In the Middle Ages there was high debate as to whether the water diviner's power came from God or the devil, but as time went on it was accepted as a good and useful faculty, and those who had the gift were much in demand, not only as water finders but also as prospectors, especially in Germany where mining for metals was highly developed and widespread. A German miner of three hundred years or so ago would carry a divining rod as part of his normal equipment, and a learned alchemist named Basilius Valentinus wrote a large tome on divining for water and metals. Some diviners of the time made what seem to us to be extravagant claims, offering to find not only water and metals but also hidden treasure, underground rooms or passages, lost or strayed animals, stolen objects, lost property and even criminals, traitors and unfaithful people, to detect lies and prove the truth, to tell how distant friends were faring and even to discover the destiny of the soul after death. A famous diviner named Jacques Aymar used his power to track down thieves and murderers, and another French diviner, Madame Ollivet of Grenoble, claimed that she could find hidden relics of saints and tell false relics from real ones. From the accounts handed down to us it seems that these and other diviners did, at least occasionally, fulfil what they claimed, but we are not told how often they failed, as against how often they succeeded, and cannot, therefore, judge how many of their successes may have been due to accident or coincidence. Some of the early diviners did not help to find a rational explanation of their craft, for they surrounded it with a lot of mystical mumbo-jumbo so as to impress the credulous and add to their own importance.

Nowadays a diviner will select his rod with some care, but always with the idea of finding the shape, size and form which will give the best practical results. In former times certain diviners tried to pass it off as a sort of magic wand, and followed queer rituals in selecting and cutting it. It must be one year's growth, and so placed in the tree or bush that the midday sun shone directly through it. It must be cut at a certain time, during the Christmas period or on Saint John's Eve or on the afternoon of Good Friday. At midnight on the Sunday after a full moon, according to others. Some held that in cutting it from the tree of bush, one should stand with one's back to it and cut it through with one stroke of the knife, while others maintained that it should be cut with three cuts in the name of the Holy Trinity while saying a prayer asking God to bless it and permit it to do good work. But some believed that evil could be worked with it, for instance that a thief could use it to open locks, and for such use it must be cut in the name of the Devil; at this stage the Old Boy himself put in an appearance and endowed the rod with all sorts of magic powers – in exchange for the soul of the would-be thief, of course. All this jiggery-pokery did not help towards a rational examination of the water diviner's strange power, and although there always were honest diviners who had no use for black magic, the efforts of a few charlatans brought a lot of disrepute on the whole art and its practitioners.

Even yet there are many people who do not believe in it, although the 'dowser' of to-day has laid aside all the old magical rites and ceremonies, and although there is a very large body of evidence to show that diviners can find water with surprising accuracy as to location, depth and volume of supply. There are many diviners in the world to-day who offer to find water for a fee, and are ready to risk their reputation on the principle of 'no water, no pay'. Sometimes an advertisment to this effect may be seen in a newspaper, and there are many cases on record where a diviner has been called in and has found a water supply where all other means have failed. Perfectly honest and sincere diviners have described their experiences in the presence of water as curious sensations running over the body and down the arms like a series of small electric shocks, and causing the rod to turn upwards or downwards in the hands with such force that they cannot keep it from doing so. These sensations sometimes are so strong that people experiencing them for the first time have been badly frightened, or have even fainted. It is said, too, that many people, as many as one in every ten or so, have this power without knowing it.

The fork-shaped rod of hazel or some other suitable natural growth is still the usual divining instrument, but some prefer a fork made of iron or copper wire, and a few use a small pendulum which swings in a certain way in the presence of water. This last may be compared with the use of a small pendulum to discover the sex of the embryo of an egg, a skill in which some country-women claim to be proficient.

Perhaps the strangest feature of all in this strange phemomenon is the claim – apparently well-founded – of some expert diviners to locate a water supply on a large scale map without visiting the locality at all. This, if fully proved, would rule out – at least in some cases – any direct influence of a body of water on the person of the diviner, and make the solution of a difficult question even more difficult still.

The Forge

Back in the old place at Easter, I walked up to the forge at the crossroads to renew an old friendship. I found that my small son had arrived already and was manfully blowing the bellows for the smith, the same bellows that I had so often blown in the old days for the father of the present smith. But there were big changes. The electric gear, the welding apparatus and the drill, were new, but where was the banding-stone gone, and the 'traveller' used to measure the circumference of a cart wheel? And all the different sizes of punches and clefts used to cut and perforate the red-hot metal, and the swages with which round bars and axles were shaped? Yes, there were a few of the old things in a dark corner of the forge, but no use for them any more, for, like everything else, the smith's job is changing. Not half the amount of work to be done, and nothing at all like the variety. A lessening number of horses to be shod, but with the shoe-iron partly shaped already, where was the skill in that? And an increasing amount of farm machinery to be repaired, but that was mostly the electric weld, or boring holes and fitting nuts and bolts, or just putting in a new spare part. Oh yes, you could make a living at it, all right, but it was more mechanic's work than blacksmithing. You could hear the tones of regret in the smith's voice as he said all this, the regret of the hereditary craftsman whose real skill and talent were so seldom required today.

In the old days it was the smith's boast that he made the tools for every tradesman, and to crown all, he also made the tools for his own trade. He made the tailor's needle and the sailor's anchor, the shepherd's crook and the forester's axe, the carpenter's saw and the thatcher's knife. Spades, pitchforks and scythes, nails, hinges and locks, handsome gates and fire-irons, griddles and brands, buckles for the harnessmaker, bands for the cooper, the weaver's lamp and the fisherman's gaff. If a housewife broke a fine 'willow-pattern' dish, the smith drilled holes in it and put it together again with stitches of iron wire. When the miller wanted a pivot for the great millstone, the smith made that, and when a little boy wanted a spear for his top, the smith made that too. There was no craftsman more busy, none more versatile, none more respected.

And he made all his own tools. The old smith used to tell us of the landlord who sent a horse to the forge with the instructions that the smith must 'make the new shoes with the old shoes, and give the old shoes to the groom riding home on the newly shod horse.' This presented no difficulty to the smith. He forged the old shoes into a hammer with which he then used to make the new shoes, and the groom took the hammer back to his master to show how it could be done. Then there was the journeyman smith who called to the forge of a smith who fancied himself and who joked the newcomer, saying that 'he supposed he was one of them fellas that could weld the six irons' – a difficult feat, that of welding six different pieces of iron together at one heating. The day wore on, but when the old smith came in after drinking his tea he found his three best pairs of tongs with their handles all welded into one solid lump, and the journeyman gone. It was some time before the old smith tried his brand of humour again on a travelling tradesman. Other difficult feats of smithcraft were the making of a horseshoe in one heating, and the making of the set of nails for one shoe in one heating.

The story is told of one Hogan, a blacksmith who had followed the Irish Brigade to France, and his encounter with Marshal de Saxe, reputed to be the strongest man in all the armies of Louis the Fifteenth. Saxe brought his horse to be shod, and when the first shoe was made he took it and pulled it straight with one jerk of his powerful hands. Hogan made a second and a third shoe, to see each of them pulled out of shape by the stranger. At last Saxe said that although the shoes were bad, they must do for his horse, as he could wait no longer, so Hogan shod the horse. Saxe handed him a louis d'or, a gold coin worth about two pounds, and Hogan bent it double between finger and thumb, with the remark that the gold they were making nowadays was just as bad as the iron, and tossed it away. The same fate met the second and third gold piece; the fourth was accepted grumblingly as better than nothing at all. Needless to say, on Saxe's departure, the bent gold coins were recovered for the smith's benefit. Another tale of strength concerns rival smiths. One of them rode past the other's forge, and stopped to ask for a light. His rival put a live coal on the anvil, and taking it by the peak in one hand reached it out of the window. The other man took the anvil in one hand and his pipe in the other and applied the live coal to the tobacco, and handed back the anvil with a word of thanks.

The local boys who met at the forge on many an evening often borrowed the anvil or the big sledgehammer for trials of strength, lifting the anvil or throwing the hammer. To grasp the sledgehammer by the end of the haft and lift it over the head with arm and hammer fully outstretched was a notable feat. 'Tossing the anvil' was another feat of strength and skill. Each contestant grasped the anvil at the peak with both hands and tried to lift it from the ground and toss it over a stick held about a yard in front and four feet high. The man who tossed it highest won. In some parts of the country tossing horseshoes was a favourite game at the forge – there always were plenty of old horseshoes lying about. But for the most part the men just stood or sat around and talked. There were always men at the forge, waiting for their turn of the smith's time – you had to wait your turn and make sure you were on the spot to get it. The forge was a regular meeting place, a sort of men's club, not only for chat and gossip, but for small business deals too, and the forge door made a handy notice board for handbills announcing letting of grazing, auctions of livestock or land, fairs and markets and the comings and goings of egglers and poultry and pig buyers.

In former times the smith made weapons as well as tools. He was the armourer of the community, turning out swords, spears and knives, lance and arrow heads, helmets and armour. Every fortress and great castle had its master smith who, with several assistants, kept the fighting men supplied. And with the coming of gunpowder many smiths became experts at making firearms, pistols and muskets, and even cannon. In later times it was the smith who armed the populance in times of insurrection. Thousands of pikes for the United Irishmen came from the forges in 1798, and many a brave smith gave his life for the cause. Again in '48 and '67 the forges were busy turning out weapons, and we hear of such famous pike-smiths as Hyland of Dublin, many of whose products are still to be seen in the National Museum and elsewhere. When a disguised policeman came to purchase in pike, in order to bring a charge against Hyland, the latter turned the tables by announcing that he had been appointed 'Pike Maker to Her Majesty the Queen'.

In ancient times the master smith was a man of high social standing. He came next after the professional class, the judges, poets, physicians and clergy, and often dined at the table of the high king. He was credited with magic powers – Saint Patrick prayed to be saved from the spells of druids, smiths and women. Special forms of tribute were paid to the smith; when the roasted animal was divided at a feast, the head always went to the smith. This custom has continued down almost to our own time; when an animal was killed, the head was sent to the local blacksmith, and there were other customary presents to the smith, corn, potatoes, vegetables and fowl, as well as such service as help in cutting turf and farm work. And the belief in the magic power of the smith is still current. The smith could loose a frightful curse against you by turning the anvil, and his capacity for healing pain and curing ailments was well-known. He was the horse doctor of the community, with treatments for farcy, glanders, spavins and all the other ills of horseflesh. He treated the cattle, too, and the dogs. He was the dentist; his method of pulling a tooth was simple

– a string from the tooth to the anvil and a red hot iron suddenly presented to the victim's nose usually did the trick. Some smiths made specially shaped forceps for pulling teeth. Water from the forge trough, in which the irons were cooled and tempered, was a notable cure for warts and for ailments of the skin.

The smith is celebrated in song and story. We have all heard of the Blacksmith of Limerick, and of Seamus O'Brien and Páid O'Donoghue. One curious tale recounts how Oliver Cromwell brought a piece of old iron to a blacksmith to be forged into a set of horseshoes – in those days the customer had to bring his own iron – but the old iron bar was a gun barrel, and when put on the fire it went off and killed Cromwell. Many tales are told of the smith's power against fairies and spirits and workers of evil magic – iron was holy and the smith himself had many strange powers. Didn't the smith refuse to make the nails used at the Crucifixion? And who made them? Why, the tinker of course, and sign's on it, isn't the tinker in misfortune ever since and the smith a respected man? And why does he never get tired? Well, a smith made a pin for Our Lady's cloak when a lazy cowherd refused to pick a long thorn for her to use as a pin, and it was then that she put the smith's weariness on the cowherd for ever.

From the earliest times the smith has been held in honour and esteem. King Conor Mac Neassa of Ulster did not disdain to dine in the house of Culann, the master smith from whom the hero Cú Chulainn got his name. And this esteem was well merited, for the material advance in culture and civilization over the centuries owes more to the blacksmith than to any other craftsman.

'Come all ye Gallant Irishmen...'

The middle of the morning at the February fair of
Newcastlewest, with a chill wind blowing the mist down
from Bearna. Farmers and their boys huddled in top or
trench coats, hands deep in pockets, ash plants under
arms, gathered in small groups, talking quietly, wishing
that the buyers – bad luck to them and their delaying!
– would get a move on and finish the business one way or
the other. The patient cattle with their heads drooped,
and the patient dogs crouched for shelter beside cart-
wheels or stout barrels. And then, suddenly, without any
introduction, the high sweet voice of a tinker girl –

> 'Twas in November, I well remember,
> Two noble hayroes to Manchester came.
> Twas their intintion, I'll freely mintion
> To free their nation from the tyrants' chain.
> The peelers viewed them and well they knew them
> And to pursue them they did not fail.
> They did surround them and in handcuffs bound
> them
> And marched them prisoners to Bellew jail!'

Heads were raised and faces turned towards the singer
and many of the men not minding the cattle drifted
towards her so that a ring of people, including several
women, gathered around her.

> 'When Allen heard that those men were taken
> To O'Brien and Larkin he quickly flew
> Saying "For Kelly and Daisey I am unaisy.
> Our comrades gone, and what can we do"?'

Verse after verse, echoing back from the tall grey houses, and at the end of every verse the comments of the audience. 'God save you the wind, girl!' 'She must be one of the O'Briens, look at the red head of her.' An old man with a beard remarked 'The Fenians were great men' and his neighbour put in with 'Well may you say it, Martin, and you one of them yourself.' The third man in the group, a much younger man, said nothing, just stood there with a faraway look in his eyes. The voice of a travelling ballad singer, and there were the old men dreaming dreams and the young men seeing visions.

That was back in the 1920's, when a ballad singer could still hold the stage. Radio was a thing of the future then, and television no more than a thought, and there still was respect for the humble artist. Nowadays the contrast is too great, the competition too severe. The ballad singer has had his day and so has the strolling musician. They are just an embarrassment now, people toss a coin to them and wish they weren't there or that they would shut up and let the world go on. Formerly you had an admiring group around every one of them at fair and pattern and hurling match from one end of the country to the other.

'Let me write a country's songs and I care not who makes its laws' said the Scottish philosopher, Fletcher of Saltoun. That the lawmakers knew the power of the poet is shown by many laws made in many countries, and not the least in our own, from the Statute of Kilkenny, made in 1366, which forbade the coming of singers, poets, storytellers, rhymers, harpers or any other Irish minstrels among the English settlers, and warned the latter not to harbour them or make gifts to them, to the mirthless and merciless judge of 1919 who sentenced a ballad singer to ten years in jail for singing the 'Peeler and the Goat', Darby Ryan's satire on the R.I.C. Of course the 'peelers', being the instrument of law nearest to ordinary people, were the butt of much mockery. In those good old days any kind of petty wrongdoing that drew the attention of the police, the unlicenced dog and the unlighted bicycle, the straying ass and the poaching of a salmon, could be advanced as acts of pure souled patriotism when the police force was, at times, misused as a force of political persecution. The ballad makers replied with such efforts as 'Bang goes the Peeler' (to the air of 'Pop goes the Weasel') and 'The Pride of Old Britannia'. Neither of these 'poems' was conspicuous for wit or humour, and few of our readers will remember them, but the 'Peeler and the Goat' is as fresh and as funny as ever.

Behind the tinker girl at the fair of Newcastle stretches a long line of itinerant poets and minstrels, reaching back into the dim recesses of the past. Much of our early history and tradition was passed on from poet to poet until it was finally written down. And in those days a poet's public was his audience – those who heard him sing or recite, or heard his songs sung or recited by others, for most people could not read, and there were few books even for those who could. So great was the power of the poet's song to praise or damn a man, and to blackmail him into parting with valuable gifts with the hope of praise or the fear of mockery, that, as we are told 'the Men of Ireland' turned against them and their expulsion was ordered, and it took the intervention of the great Saint Colmcille to save them from banishment over the sea. Colmcille was himself a poet, and we know from his poems that he had felt the bitterness of exile. No wonder then that he put in a good word for the poets and saved them; they had to give a promise of good behaviour, which they kept, no doubt, as long as they had to.

Every Irish lord had his poets, whose main duty it was to make poems in praise of himself and his family, and to sing them on every possible occasion. The Normans were not long settled in Ireland before they had adopted the Irish fashion, and not only had court poets but themselves composed poems in Irish and in the Irish measures. That they sang in Norman-French and in English, too, we know. One of the earliest documents about the Normans in Ireland is a long poem in praise of Dermot MacMurrough and the first of the Norman invaders, said to have been made by one Maurice Regan who was Dermot's interpreter. This poem describes Dermot as brave, generous, noble, rich and powerful, and must have given much satisfaction to him and to his son-in-law, Strongbow, and brought many a coin into the pouch of the minstrels who sang it in camp and in castle. But the Normans and their Minstrels had light and merry songs, too, treating of love and gay adventure, or of the minor sadnesses of life –

'Harrow! jeo soy trahy
Par fol amour de mal amy!'
'Woe is me! I am undone
by foolish love for a faithless one!'

Over the east and south of Ireland the Irish and the Norman tradition mingled to give new life to poem and ballad, just as at a later stage, in the 18th and 19th centuries, the introduction of English and Lowland Scottish songs brought a similar mingling of traditions in popular ballad making and singing, with songs like 'Barbara Allen' and 'Uncle Rat went out to ride' and 'Green Brooms,' and many English and Scottish airs, many singers not knowing – or caring – whether the song they were singing was Irish, English or Scottish.

One interesting aspect of this mingling of tradition was the carrying over of Irish (Gaelic) forms of verse and metre into English speech, especially the rhyming of stressed syllables throughout the stanza: –

> 'There's statues gracing that lovely place in,
> Of gods and pagans and nymphs so fair.
> Of Plutarch, Vaynus and Nicodaymus
> All standing naked in the open air!
> And now to end my brief narration
> Which my poor jaynus could not entwine.
> But if I were Ceasar or Nebuchodnaser
> 'Tis in every fayture I'd make it shine!'

That song, 'The Groves of Blarney', was written as a skit upon the ballad-makers, but is just the kind of thing to be found in dozens of ballads of the last century. There were songs with every second line or every second verse in Irish and English, and translations or versions of Irish songs, made over into English, often with the last line still in Irish repeated at the end of each verse –

> 'I would toil the long years of my life
> Through storm, through sunshine and rain.
> I would venture the battle's red strife
> For to save her one moment of pain.
> I would climb the high hills of the land,
> I would swim to the depths of the sea

For one touch of her lily-white hand.
Ach ar Éirinn ní neósainn cé h-í.'

There was one big difference between the songs made
and sung locally and those that formed the stock in
trade of the 'professional' ballad singer, for the ballad-
singer had to attract and hold an audience in the open
air and move them to contribute their pennies to his hat
or to buy a broadsheet. A local song might not be understood outside the parish, but the song to draw a
crowd at the fair or the races must appeal to everybody,
and tell of some well-known event or praise some popular cause. And shyness did not help the street singer; he
(or she, for many of them were women) must catch the
crowd at the first line. That is why so many of them
begin with 'Come all ye lads and lasses' or 'Come all ye
faithful Irishmen', so that a 'come-all-ye' came to be
another name for a street ballad.

'Come all ye sporting heroes and listen unto me,
I pray you give attention, whoever ye may be.
Till I sing about a boxing-match that was held the
other day
Between a Russian sailor and gallant Morrisy.'

and so on, describing forty-two rounds of a barefist
fight, with a long introduction and conclusion fore and
aft, at least fifty verses. Time was less important in those
days than now, and your modern song of three verses
wouldn't loosen a ballad singer's throat.

At the end of the song the ballad singer went around in
the crowd, selling the broadsheets. 'Buy the new ballet!
Only a pinny each the ballets!!' Usually the sale was
brisk, for people loved to sing and this was almost the
only way in which new songs reached the countryside.

And not only the 'come-all-yes' appeared on the ballad sheets, but also, in their day, the lyrics of Thomas Moore and Robert Burns and the patriotic songs of Davis, Kickham and the writers of the 'Nation'. In the later 19th century there was a flood of 'stage-Irishman' songs, like 'The Garden where the Praties Grow', 'Bridget Donohue' and 'The Whistling Thief', most of them by known authors. And so on through the gay songs of Percy French to our own day, when the last weak effort of the ballad singers is dying away.

The ballad singers, like the authors of many of their songs, have left few names behind. Dublin can boast of 'Zozimus', the blind singer whose real name was Michael Moran and who used to take his stand on one of the bridges over the Liffey and entertain the passing crowds. He composed his own songs, but only a few fragments are remembered – a source of regret when we hear the first verse of his famous 'Finding of Moses': –

> 'In Aygipt's land, contagious to the Nile
> Ould Pharaoh's daughter went to bathe in style.
> She took her dip and came unto the land,
> And for dry her royal pelt she ran along the strand.
> She tripped upon a bulrush and she saw
> An infant lying on a wad of straw.
> She gazed upon it, and in accents mild
> Said "Tare an' ages, gerrils, which of yiz owns the
> child?".'

Probably we shall never learn what literary gems are hidden in the subsequent verses.

The ballad singer's day is gone. Who would be so foolhardy as to raise his voice in song, in the hope of reward, at the fancy dress parades that have taken the

place of the old come-as-you-please gatherings? Or
burst into melody at a cattle mart? But while we drink
in the slickly doled out ration of 'pops' and classics that
surges from our loudspeakers, let us sometimes spare a
kindly thought for all the unknown artists who lightened
our grandfather's day with their songs.

The Faction Fighters

It is quite commonplace, nowadays, to say that the old ways and traditions are dying out. Of course they are. The impact of modern development, with its new materials and methods, with its rapid transport and almost instant passage of information across the face of the world, is profoundly changing the lives of ordinary men and women in every land under the sun. Ireland is no exception, and we would not have it one; we have reached a stage, let us hope, when we can select and preserve the best features of our past to light our future. But the second half of the last century and the first decades of this saw a very curious influence – Victorianism – at work with disastrous results for many aspects of Irish tradition. The essence of Victorianism was, of course, 'respectability', and this 'respectability' attained the status of a moral code for far too many people. It wasn't 'respectable' to be a Fenian, for instance. It wasn't 'respectable' to eat porridge or oaten bread or salt herrings, and these and many similar items passed out of the diet of the country people. It wasn't 'respectable' to make the rounds at the blessed well, and clergy and laity alike combined to suppress most of the Patterns. And, above all, faction fighting was a cause of horror to the 'respectables', and, even after the lapse of a century, is still regarded askance by people whose great-grandfathers trounced each other through fair and market in many a hard fought battle.

In reality faction fighting was nothing more than a

crude and dangerous form of sport. And here we must
not exaggerate either its crudity or its danger. It was no
more crude than boxing or all-in wrestling is nowadays,
and, as to its danger, the number of people killed and
crippled in any year was not at all as great as that produced by the dangerous sport of to-day, namely car
driving. The list of killed and injured in road accidents
which we read in small paragraphs in our daily paper,
and dismiss as one of the normal hazards of our time
would have shocked the nation if they had been caused,
a century ago, by faction fighting.

To the fighters themselves it was an expert game, a
form of stick fencing. Incidentally, the so-called
'shillelaghs' which are sold to tourists nowadays are not
the faction fighter's weapon, and do not seem to have
any traditional background in Ireland; they are, rather,
the chosen weapon of the London tough, the Bill Sykes
of Dickens' time. The faction fighters used an ordinary
ashplant or blackthorn walking stick. Admittedly it was
chosen and prepared with care, but it was to all intents
and purposes a walking-stick, about three feet long. The
fighter grasped it about one third of its length from the
ferule end, and the projecting foot or so of the stick
served to protect his arm and elbow from his opponents
blows, while the longer portion covered his head and
body. Some were very expert and spent long hours
practising every trick of stick fencing in mock fights with
a friend or in real duels with selected opponents. The
story is told of a young man about to set out for the fair of
Ardagh when his old father, telling him to guard himself, twisted the young man's stick out of his hand with
a quick twirl of his own. 'There you are now boy! Didn't

I tell you not to close your thumb over your fingers? Up along the stick you should put your thumb, to give you power over it'. Often the expert fighter struck for the funny bone, thus temporarily paralysing his opponent's arm without injuring him, for a small tap was enough.

The main factions of the middle of County Limerick were the 'Three Year Olds' and the 'Four Year Olds', who are said to have got their names from a fight arising out of an argument over the age of a beast at the Fair of the Well in Ballyagran. In east Limerick there was the Coffeys and the Riaskawallas, and the Caravats and Shanavests, while on the Kerry Border the big factions were the Cooleens and the Black Mulvihils. But there were numerous local factions, some of them identified with certain families or family names, such as the Collinses and the Macks, or the Hartnets and the McInirys. The names of some of the notable leaders are still remembered, like Séamus Mór Hartnet who squeezed water out of the head of a blackthorn that had been seasoning up the chimney for seven years, or Connor Cregan who broke his stick at the fair of Newcastlewest and rearmed himself by pulling the shaft out of a sidecar and breaking it to a suitable length over his knee.

The proceedings usually started with a challenge. One man – a faction leader – called out the other side. In some places he 'trailed his coat' and his opponent took up the challenge by standing on it. In other places the custom was to carry two sticks and offer his choice to the opponent. But the usual custom in County Limerick – and in most of Munster was 'wheeling'. The champion stood out and 'wheeled' his stick over his head, shouting his own or his faction's war cry: –

'Cúilín mise agus cá bhfuil fear mo theangabhála?'

'Here's a real Three Yeal Old!'

'Who'll stand against a Hartnet?'

'Up the Blacks and who'll say boo to a Mulvihil?'

Seldom did the challenge pass unanswered and soon the fight became general. People unconcerned with the result left the street or the fair ground without delay, and the contestants often fought for an hour or more before one faction was driven from the field or took refuge in houses or under carts, from which they might be driven by the elated victors. Of course bystanders could join in if they felt like a bit of sport. Witness the case of the stalwart young man who was asked to which faction he belonged, and who replied courteously, 'Neither side, indeed, but I'd like a bit of a puck around, if ye have no objection' or the polite little girl who pulled the coat tails of a gentleman busily occupied in beating the lard out of another gentleman, with the question 'Excuse me, sir, but me da wants to know is it private or can he join in?' Even women took a hand at times. As one old lady, fondly remembering the days of her youth, put it – 'It would be the cold-hearted woman that wouldn't come to the help of her man or her boy and he in the thick of the fight'. The women did not handle sticks; their weapon was a stout woollen stocking with a stone weighing a pound or so in the toe of it. A man was at a disadvantage when faced by one of these Amazons, he might parry her blows, but on no account must he hit her. On the other hand, the women seldom interfered unless their menfolk were being badly defeated.

There were, of course, casualties. Occasionally there were deaths, and a fight seldom passed without some serious injuries. The learned Dr. Sylvester O'Halloran writes in the preface of his *Treatise on the Head:* 'During the course of twenty years' practice I have never been a month without half a dozen broken heads coming under my inspection, and one or two skulls to trepan, that had been caused by fighting.'

Many customs and conventions were observed. There was fair fighting, man against man, and dirty fighting, where several men set upon one man, or where a by-stander struck one of a pair engaged in single combat; such an interloper might get a good blow in return from his own champion who would resent the implication of foul play. And the matter of loyalty followed a pattern. Each family and each townland had its own allegiance. A servant boy or a workman was supposed to side with his employer, and – curiously enough – a married man must support the faction of his wife's family wherever his former loyalty had lain.

The great fighters are gone this hundred years and their dust is lying in Kilfergus and Templeathea, Rath-cahill and Rathnasaer. They were men of their time and, though it all seems very foolish to us now, they admired strength and skill and courage. We could do worse than they, and we certainly have no cause to be ashamed of them.

Haste to the Wedding

One of my earliest memories is that of seeing a wedding party going the road. It was on a late July morning in that warm, lovely summer of 1921 when the Truce had lifted the fear from the people's minds and when hearts were high. There were eight horse-cars in the cavalcade; six of them were traps, with a back-to-back and a side-car. Coming back from the church they were, to the bride's parents' house, at a fast trot with little puffs of dust rising from the horses' hoofs. In the first trap were the bride and the bridegroom, with the bridesmaid and the best man, in the second the bride's father and mother and sisters, with the other relations and friends following on behind. On the way to the church before the wedding the order was somewhat different; the bride and her parents were in the first trap, while the bridegroom was in the last of all. Of course the thirty-odd people in this procession were by no means the only wedding guests, for this was in the good old days when everybody in the townland was expected at the wedding, and the failure to appear there of at least one person from each household might be regarded as a slight on the bride's family, unless there was some good reason for it. We children went along as well as the next; there was no school to distract us – the bridegroom, indeed, was a schoolmaster making good use of his summer holidays. For us the rest of the day was a blur of singing and dancing and other grown-up merry-making, frequently

punctuated by sweets, oranges, jellies and other important matters with which a younger daughter of the
house thoughtfully kept us provisioned.

A century earlier the party would not have gone to
the church at all. Instead, the priest would have come to
the house and performed the ceremony there. In those
days the wedding celebration was held in the house in
which the young couple would live, which was usually
the young man's (or his parents) house, sometimes the
bride's house, if the man were 'marrying in' there. In
those days, too, the procession was from the bride's
parents' home to that of the bridegroom, in cars or
carts, on foot, or – oftenest – on horseback with the
women carried on pillions behind the men, with her
father or elder brother carrying the bride. Often the
young men raced furiously across country from one
house to the other, and expected to be rewarded with
bottles of liquor. Even when the church ceremony became usual this mad race was sometimes run from the
house to the church and back again after the ceremony;
the old people still tell of the sad day when three riders
collided outside the gate of the church in Knocknagoshel,
and a young friend of the groom was thrown and killed.
Arrived at the house about mid-morning the party were
bidden to fall to upon the good things spread out. Often
there was not room in the house for the throng, and
tables were laid in the barn, or even in the farmyard.
Often, too, if it was known that a very large crowd
would gather, tactful neighbours had helped things on
with presents of fowl, bacon, bread, cakes and beverages,
for any appearance of shortage or niggardliness at a
wedding was a source of shame for all concerned, and

might be 'thrown up against them' by some ill-inten-
tioned person at a fair or a market years afterwards.

Usually the merrymaking was directed by a friend of
the groom, acting as a sort of master of ceremonies. He
marshalled the musicians and kept them suitably lubri-
cated, and called for the next song or dance as occasion
arose. The fun was well under way by the time the priest
arrived. It was demanded by custom that the priest
should stay on at the party after the marriage, and so his
other parish duties for the day must have been already
performed. Needless to day the Parish Clerk was in
attendance, full of importance, and to all outward
seeming much more concerned with the proper order of
things than the pastor himself. On the priest's coming all
music and noise was stilled, and the guests crowded into
the kitchen to see the couple joined. The ceremony
over, the priest called for witnesses, and many pressed
forward to have the honour of being recorded by name.
You may still find in old parish registers entries such as
'... Testes fuerunt Thaddeus Ahern, Mauritius Fitz-
maurice, Johanna Murphy, Jacobus Roche, Gulielmus
O'Connor, Maria Woulfe cum multis aliis', giving the
names of five or six witnesses and adding that there were
many others present. Then the priest was given a place
of honour; if he were known to be a signer or a musician,
he was at a later stage requested by the groom or one of
the older people to entertain the company with a song or
a tune. In this connection the old people still kept the
memory of Father Patrick Ahern as a sweet singer and
an expert violin player – the parish clerk brought the
violin with the vestments. Father Ahern was killed by a
fall from his horse when returning at night from a sick-

call in the year 1804, but a hundred and twenty years later the people still spoke of him as if he had left the parish only the month before.

A man should never sing at his own wedding. Neither should his bride. But they were expected to take part in the first dance, with the best man and the bridesmaid. After that, dance followed dance, interspersed with songs or tunes. Step dancers were in demand – especially such experts as the man who used to dance a hornpipe on the head of a sixteen-gallon keg.

There always was drink in plenty at a wedding, although any sign of drunkenness was regarded as an insult to the people of the house and the married pair. One man, a friend of the family, was appointed to see after the drink and distribute it as needed; he was expected to know everybody's taste, and to press them to drink heartily. In former times the only drinks – besides milk – were whiskey and wine, later porter and tea became the most usual, although whiskey and wine were still to the fore, and many an old man or woman was heard to say 'Ah, sure I have the pledge! I'll have a half of wine!'

No wedding was complete without the visit of at least one group of strawboys, or 'soppers' as we called them, although they had laid aside the straw cloaks and masks formerly worn, and were disguised in old clothes, their faces blackened with burnt cork or soot. They seldom came before the fall of night, and they always included a musician in their number. They never entered a house unless invited to do so by the groom or his father, but the invitation was always given, for to turn them away was unheard of. After all, they were neighbour's sons, and, besides, their coming was taken as a token of the esteem for the married pair and their people. Usually there were six or eight in the group, and when they were admitted their leader went straightaway to the bride, wished her joy and asked her to dance, while three of his companions asked three other girls, and they all danced an eight hand reel to their own music. The dance finished they were treated to drinks all round. It was a point of honour that the company should recognise them, in spite of the disguise, and if there happened to be a noted singer or dancer among them he was asked to entertain the guests. Then they raised a loud cheer for the bride and groom and took their leave. Often, at Shrovetide, there were a dozen or more weddings in the parish, and the soppers made their way to the next wedding party, and often there were several groups of them on their rounds. Incidentally, on such a day of many weddings the parish priest was a busy man, calling at house after house to perform the ceremonies, and it might be well after nightfall before the last couple were joined.

That was the heyday of the matchmakers. In some places there were recognised matchmakers who – for a consideration – were prepared to act as go-between. More usually the matter was arranged by the parents or friends of the young couple meeting at fair or market and repairing to the back room of the village pub to thresh the matter out, with long discussions on the merits of the boy and girl and much argument over the dowry and other details of the marriage settlement. In our part of the country, however, the first steps were taken by some friends of the young man visiting the girl's house and 'drawing down' the match with her parents. The favourite time for such visits was 'between Big and Little Christmas,' with a view to a wedding the following Shrove. In a farming community it was necessary that there should be economic and social parity between the boy and the girl, hence the matchmaking, and hence the long discussion on the dowry and the man's expectations. If he had the grass of twenty cows it was understood that the 'fortune' should be greater than he might expect if he had the grass of only ten. It was expected, too, that the friends of the girl would visit the man's farm and see the quality of the land and the evidence of his husbandry. 'Walking the land' is what that was called, and the visiting party must be well entertained in the young man's home – any lack of hospitality or any sign of meanness counted heavily against the success of the venture. Tales are told of matches made without the young people's knowledge, but more usually the parties mainly concerned had the right of refusal if the match did not appeal to them, and frequently there already was an understanding between them, and the friends who came to make the match knew of it.

In the old days, before the Famine, people married young, and a young couple expected to be guided and advised by their elders both before and after the marriage. Indeed, neither man nor woman reached full status in the rural community until they were married. The unmarried were still 'boys' and 'girls' even up to their old age, and a married woman of twenty-one had a much more important position in life than a spinster of fifty. The same held good for the men. All this was acceptable when people did marry young; to see a young married man advised and guided by his parents was edifying, but as the nineteenth century went on, and marriages were entered upon later and later in life, the sight of a 'boy' of close on fifty being ordered about by a doddering old parent was by no means a reassuring spectacle. In one such case an old friend of mine tried to persuade an elderly woman that her only son, aged forty-nine, might be better settled down in life. 'Yerra, hould your whist!' was her reply, 'Wouldnt another tin years be great hardening in him?'

Matchmaking did not always run smoothly. There was the case, not a hundred miles from the Kerry Border, where the boy and the girl were agreed, and the boy's family were all for the match, but her old father was a tough customer and hard to pin down. Three times the match seemed to be made, and three times broken by his obstinacy, until, at length, the boy's mother called on the parish priest to tell him that everything was arranged and the day set. 'Tell me, ma'am' said the priest, 'how ever did you get round old Johnny?' 'Well, to tell you the truth, father, we told a few of the boys to go over and fire a few shots outside the house to show him that we were in earnest.' There are always ways and means to smooth the course of love.

Marriage was the wished-for destiny of the young people. It meant a settled life and a degree of independence unknown outside of it. Many and wonderful were the means of divination employed, especially by girls, to discover who their future partners might be. And all sorts of signs and portents were observed on the wedding day. A fine day meant luck especially if the sun shone on the bride; a day of rain foretold hardship. It was unlucky to marry on a Saturday, and those who married in harvest would spend all their lives gathering. A man should always be the first to wish joy to the bride, never a woman, although we hear of cases where jealous or spiteful women tried to bring bad luck on a marriage by forestalling the man. It was lucky to hear a cuckoo on the wedding morning, or to see three magpies. To meet a funeral on the road meant bad luck, and if there was a funeral on that day, the wedding party on the way to the groom's house, or to or from the church always took a different road. The wedding day was a big day for the whole townland, and nothing should be allowed to cast a shadow over it.

The Hedge School

About ten years ago an old schoolmaster down in County Limerick told me this story from his childhood: – 'I remember one evening – it would be in 1884, in the month of November – when I ran home from school to my grandmother's house. It was cold and misty and I was hungry, with nothing in my head but the thought of a big plate of pandy and butter and a wedge of the Hallow E'en applecake. Coming in through the yard I heard the excited voices talking Irish inside, and when I came to the kitchen door I saw my grandmother and old Aunty Norry sitting at the fire with an old, old priest whose head was as white as snow. They never noticed me; they were lost in the memories of long ago, and I soon forgot my hunger listening to them. In time I got my supper, but I sat up until late intent on the conversation. It was then I heard this incident from a vanished world.

'A night school used to be held in the house of my grandmother's father, Tom Culhane of Riddlestown. The teachers were a poor scholar, who used to live with them, and the local curate, Father Darby Egan. They studied Latin and Greek as well as Mathematics, English and other subjects; the priest it was who taught the Latin. One night he finished a book of Virgil with them and was telling them the story of the next book they would begin the following night. Then the class broke up and the boys went off home. One of them, a lad named

Connors, lived a couple of miles away, and before he got home he was arrested by a patrol of soldiers and dragged off to the jail in Limerick as a suspected Whiteboy. There was little justice in those days, and the best he could hope for was to be pressed into the British Navy, to save his neck from the rope, for the war against Napoleon was on then, and many an accused man was given that choice, so as to fill the ranks. Word came back to Culhane's, and the woman of the house, my greatgrandmother – her name was Mary Mulcahy, Tom Culhane's wife – put on her cloak and went straight up to the Landlord's house, where she was a good friend of the housekeeper, and so got speech with the landlord, Mr Blennerhasset. He was an important man, a magistrate and a member of the Grand Jury, and sure enough, he took Tom Culhane into Limerick with him next day and procured young Connors' release. The same night the school was in session again when Tom Culhane returned in triumph bringing young Connors with him, and when all the handshaking and congratulations were over the woman of the house demanded that young Connors should tell all his adventures. He swept off his hat and bowed low to her, saying 'Infandum Regina jubes renovare dolorem!' Everyone laughed at that, because it was the first line of the new book of Virgil, what the hero said when the Queen asked him to tell of his adventures. And the old priest who came to visit my grandmother was the same young Connors, returned after many years in the American mission.'

The old schoolmaster who told this tale is, like all the others concerned, now dead. God rest them all. But the little picture of the past remains bright and clear. The

old thatched farmhouse with the bright fire in the kitchen. The priest and the poor scholar vieing with each
other in learning. The little circle of attentive young
men. The farmer's children listening and picking up a bit
of the classics here and there – they had had their lessons
in the three R's from the poor scholar earlier in the day.
The flow of erudition, Latin, Greek, Rhetoric, Philosophy and Mathematics. The farmer and his good wife
looking on in admiration and the servant boys and girls
amazed at so much wisdom. And there was nothing
unusual in all this, for similar gatherings could be found
in many farmhouses up and down the country.

How did this come about? In the Middle Ages the
monasteries dispensed learning to all who sought it, and
in the larger towns there were schools conducted by
clerics or laymen. Then came the Reformation, and the
enemies of the old religion saw a great as menace to their
plans in the schoolmaster as in the friar or the Jesuit. He
too, they determined, must go. But the people loved
learning, and devoted teachers were ready to risk liberty
and even life in following their vocation. The hunt began
under Henry VIII, yet over a hundred years later we
find the Cromwellians fulminating against 'Popish
Schoole Masters' who were teaching the Irish youth
'trayning them up in Supersticion, Idolatry and the
Evill Customs of the Nacion' and making orders that
such schoolmasters are to be secured and shipped to
slavery in the Barbadoes. The cloud lifted for a brief
period under James II, but the mismanagement of that
unfortunate monarch ended with the second Siege of
Limerick, and the Penal Laws clamped down more
heavily than ever on popular education; for nearly

another hundred years the school and the schoolmaster
– as far as Catholics were concerned – were completely
outlawed. 'Universal, unqualified, and unlimited pro-
scription' is how the historian Lecky described the laws
against education. Heavy fines and long terms of impri-
sonment or transportation to the colonies were prescribed not only for the schoolmaster but also for anyone who
sheltered him or any friendly landlord or magistrate who
tried to shield him. Rewards were freely offered – and
paid – to informers, and any person over the age of
sixteen could be brought before a court and examined
on oath about suspected schools. Even heavier penalties
awaited those who tried to send their sons abroad to
schools on the Continent, and few could afford the cost
of this. Clerical students braved the wrath of the law to
reach the Irish colleges in Louvain, Paris, Salamanca
and Rome, and the smugglers' boats carried not only
the recruits for the Irish regiments in France and Spain
but also the young men ready to risk all for the priest-
hood. But these boys had to have some grounding in
education, and there were the thousands to whom a bit
of learning was as important as their daily bread. How
were they to get it? The hidden school, the 'hedge-
school', was the answer.

A small low hut, as inconspicuous as possible, was built
in some place sheltered from view, and in it the hunted
schoolmaster taught his class. There might be no door or
windows, just openings in the wall; there might not even
be room to stand up inside, but secrecy was necessary,
and the more like an old cattle shed the safer. There was
too much risk to the household in running a school in a
farmhouse, and the school building was a poor hovel at

best, so whenever it was not raining the master and his class sat under the shelter of a hedge out of doors. Hence the name. The boys took turns to act as sentries, one or two at a time watching out for any strangers who might be a danger to the school. In wet weather they sat in the hut, not at all as comfortably as under the hedge on a fine day. In winter there might be a fire around which the children took turns to sit, especially the smaller ones.

What did they learn? Reading, writing and arithmetic were then, as now, regarded as the basis of schooling. Reading and spelling of English was the first task to which the small children were set, and they learned by 'rehearsing', that is by repeating the lesson all together, from the 'Rational Spelling Book', the 'Hibernian Preceptor' or 'Reading Made Easy', three popular lesson books. William Carleton, at the age of six, learned the whole alphabet and a few simple spellings, like b-a-g bag, on his first day at the hedge school, and Daniel O'Connell did even better, for when he was only four years old he learned the alphabet, once and for all, from a hedge schoolmaster named Mahony, in an hour and a half. Slightly older children were taught writing and figures, first on slates – which, with the pencils, were home made, and later with paper and quill pens. Voster's arithmetic was the usual text book for figures; this was superseded later by Bonnycastle's and Deighan's. The older children, and young men and women up almost to the age of twenty, went on to algebra, geometry, rhetoric, Latin and Greek. Classical learning was highly regarded. 'I have known many poor men, such as broom-sellers, car-drivers and day-labourers who could speak Latin with considerable fluency' wrote a Killarney schoolmaster in 1808 to an English scholar of his acquaintance; in actual fact his letter is in Latin, as more suiting the dignity of a scholar.

The master was paid by the parents, at so much per child per quarter, from about 1/6 or 2/- for the small ones learning reading and writing to ten or twelve shillings for the young men learning the Classics. But with small classes and poor clients the master was lucky if he made forty pounds a year – 'passing rich' as Goldsmith says. Of course this was not all his income, for he got many presents from grateful parents, such as potatoes, butter, fowl, pieces of bacon, turf and milk. He also made something on the side, by writing letters, drawing up wills, preparing petitions and other documents or keeping accounts for a fee. There is the case of a master of about 1860 – a National Teacher by now – whose spare-time job as land steward to a big farmer paid him once-and-a-half as much as his salary as a teacher. Sometimes there was a default in payment; the parents were not satisfied with the teacher or were too mean or too poor to pay, and the master could lament, like Mícheál Ó Longáin in West Limerick –

'Is ainis mo ghnó a's is róbhocht dealbh mo shlí
Ag teagasc na n-óg a's ní fónta meastar me dhíol.
Ach geallaimse dhóibh, gac lóma fleascaigh sa tír
Gura fada go ngeóidh mo shórtsa eatartha arís!'

('Miserable is my business and most poor my lot, instructing the young and not being honestly paid. But I promise to them, to each rustic boor in the land, that long will it be until my like comes among them again.') Such verses were sung far and wide, to the discomfiture of those who had wronged the master, for, like the poets of old, the hedge schoolmasters used satire as a sharp and dreaded weapon, and one against which there was little defence. There were times when the satire recoiled upon the master, as when a young woman, mocked in verse by Donnchadh Rua Mac Conmara, set fire to the school and forced the master to fly for his life: such extreme measures were rare, however, for usually the master was highly esteemed in the community, and few had the temerity to 'cross' him. It must be admitted, however, that there were masters who failed to keep up the high standards expected, as when the rakish Eoin Rua O'Sullivan was engaged to instruct certain young ladies, and was found, alas!, to have carried his teaching too far, with the result that he had to fly the district and take refuge as a recruit in the British navy.

In the second half of the eighteenth century the laws against education were relaxing, and in many districts they were not rigorously applied by kindly magistrates or lenient landlords. With more settled conditions there were many decent Protestants growing more and more disgusted with the indignities heaped upon their Catholic fellow-Irishmen, and in 1782 the 'Volunteer Parliament' passed an Act which gave Catholics some freedom to teach schools and attend them. But this did not end the days of the hedge schools; it meant that they were no longer illegal, but it did not mean that school buildings and other facilities were provided overnight. In some places, especially in the towns, it was not long until school buildings appeared, and clerics, nuns and layfolk taught openly and with general satisfaction. But as we might expect, there were many country places where the only change was that the school could now be

held in a farmhouse kitchen or other such place without
risk to the owners. Often the older boys had to work
during the day, and did their lessons at night, hence the
'night school', a direct offshoot of the hedge school.
Often a farmer gave a barn or a large byre over as a
school, and stools, desks and blackboards began to appear. Printers could now produce schoolbooks in numbers, and some of the 'chapbooks' sold cheaply and used
as reading books look rather odd to us today, titles such
as 'Freeny the Robber', 'Famous Rogues and Rapparees',
'The Devil and Doctor Faustus', 'The History of Witches
and Apparitions', and others even more unsuitable.

Some of these schools are the direct ancestors of well-
known schools of today; others just died out when better
schools were established. But in remote parts of the
country such humble sources of learning kept on working even into the present century, and there are people
still alive who can honestly claim to have received their
first lessons in a hedge school.

The Wake

Sometimes the soc of a plough lifts a capstone from an ancient grave and shows us with what reverence our remote ancestors buried their dead. The position of the skeleton in the stone-lined tombs shows that the body was placed there lying on its side and curled up as if asleep; close by are stone or bronze weapons and tools and jars which contained food or drink, gifts for the departed one and provisions for his future life. We can imagine that the dead man was dressed in his best and that the tools and weapons laid in the grave with him were his favourite ones. We can expect, too, that many objects and articles of wood, leather and cloth were included, that have now quite decayed away. We do not know what our distant ancestors believed about the after life, and we can only vaguely guess at what strange ceremonies attended the burial, but we can see clearly that they did believe in a continuing existence after death, and were moved by the two considerations which still affect us, that is grief and regret at the departure of a dear friend or relative, and provision for his future life.

The people's notions about death were set right by the teachings of Christianity – the soul had returned to its Maker and the body, now deserted by the soul, should be laid away with reverence. But the old pagan ideas were very different, if we can judge by the beliefs and customs of primitive pagan tribes in far-off corners of the world in recent times. According to these, the dead continue in an existence very similar to that which they enjoyed on earth. Many of the American Indians believed in the 'Happy Hunting Grounds' to which the dead went if they had been upright and brave, and where life was one long round of manly sports, where game abounded and where a man's only task was to display his prowess in the chase to his admiring women-folk. Thus, when a warrior died, he must be provided with the best of weapons and the gayest of robes, feathers and beadwork that he might maintain his dignity and station. We know that many peoples of Europe, the Vikings for example, had much the same belief, and the best of everything, even ships and wagons, should be sent with their dead chieftains to Valhalla. Some people went farther; the dead man's wives, retainers and slaves were killed and buried with him, that he might lack no state or comfort.

Other peoples believed that the dead remained close at hand and continued to interest themselves in the affairs of the living, either helpfully or harmfully. The Chinese held that the dead were happy only as long as there living relatives and descendants continued to offer them food and other signs of care and respect. Should the supply fail, the departed ancestors might make their displeasure felt in a variety of unpleasant ways; on the other hand, if they were flattered by plenteous offerings, they ensured that the living were protected from all calamity. But other peoples, especially in less civilised regions, thought that the dead were spitefully or evilly inclined – they had left the good things of this life for a poorer, more miserable sphere and were only too ready to air their feelings if suitable presents were not forthcoming. So if any ill-luck befel a man, his first thought was 'Now, which of my dead kinsmen is angry'?, and away he went with an offering to the appointed place. If the bad luck held, he had guessed wrongly and must try to placate another ancestor. Some unfortunate tribes were bothered, badgered and bedevilled by the spirits of their dear departed constantly demanding the best of everything. Others worked out the convenient theory that only the last person to die must be so cajoled, and this reduced the number of offerings considerably. In parts of New Guinea the skull of the most recently dead relative was kept in a place of honour in the house, and offered food and comforts like any member of the family, but when the next person died, the other was removed and the new skull put in the place of honour.

It is probable that different groups of our Pagan forebears held different views about the dead. Some of them, perhaps, thought that their deceased friends had departed to happier place – call it Tír na nÓg, if you like. Others believed, maybe, that the dead had gone no further away than the place of burial, and must still be treated with cautious reverence lest they resent indifference or undue interference. Then came Christianity to change all their notions of this life and the next, but we can be sure that many of the old beliefs and customs were kept in use, either with the consent of the Church or in spite of it. This explains certain practices which have come down almost to our own time; some of them may seem very peculiar but they all come from the same motives, respect for the dead and a desire to help them, and respect for the living relatives and a desire to help them, too. It is in that light we must judge these customs no matter how strange they appear.

In several regions in Ireland there was a belief, very strongly held, that the last person to be buried in a graveyard must act as a sort of servant to all the other dead in the place. Sometimes specific tasks are mentioned, such as bringing water every night from a nearby well. This belief often lead to undignified scenes if two funerals approached the place at the same time, for each hurried the corpse ahead to try and get it into the burial place first. Some people went so far as to try to prevent by force the entry of the others, and cases are recorded where a free fight developed between the two funeral parties. Other strange beliefs are reflected by the remark of an old County Limerick farmer in his last illness who looked out the window towards Knockfierna, the fairy hill, and said 'Twon't be long now till I'm in there with the rest of them', or the other man who, before he turned away from the grave of an old crony, pushed a shilling under the sod as a last offering to his friend.

From the moment of death until the burial tradition demanded that the body should never be left alone and unwatched. There were many reasons for this, principally respect and affection for the one who had died. There was also some degree of fear of supernatural intervention. And during some centuries – up to a hundred years or so ago – body snatchers were always ready to steal an unguarded corpse and sell it to the medical schools which were foolishly prevented from getting material for instruction in legitimate ways. And the body should not be watched by a lone person; strength in numbers was the keynote here. When going to or coming from a wake one should not be alone; at least two went together, and it was better still if people went in groups.

Since nearly everybody in the parish wished to pay their respects to the dead, there usually was a fairly big crowd of people at the wake, and as some went away others came. On entering the house the visitors first knelt beside the corpse and said a prayer, then offered condolences to the relatives before joining the main body of mourners. Of course the whole feeling of the wake depended upon the circumstances of the death. If a worthy old person had died at an advanced age, it was proper to do all the right things, but the degree of grief and tragedy was not at all as great as when, say, a young father or mother had died leaving little orphans, or when the strong young son of helpless parents had been killed in an accident. In these latter cases there was genuine sorrow and compassion and nothing was said or done which might upset the relatives, but where it was the expected death of an old person, the event was more of a social occasion, an opportunity to meet friends, in some cases almost a celebration or party, at which stories were told, songs were sung and games played.

At the moment of death the clock was stopped; this is said to have been done so that all could see the actual time of death, for which people usually made enquiry. The body was decently laid out on a table in the largest room – sometimes in the barn, and not in a bedroom as is usual now. Lighted candles were placed near and a dish of snuff laid beside the corpse, sometimes on the corpse's chest. Everybody who came should take a pinch and say a prayer for the repose of the dead. Large numbers of new clay pipes already filled with tobacco were put in charge of a neighbour, whose task it was to see that every man who came got a pipe, and every man must light up and take a few puffs whether a smoker or not. Any woman who wished to smoke also got a pipe, and many of the old ladies were not behindhand in this, while the younger women contented themselves with the pinch – or several pinches – of snuff. In some places the residue of the snuff was put away with care to be used as a cute for headaches. There are places, too, where the left-over pipes were placed on the grave, but usually any material left over, whether food, drink, tobacco or snuff was given either to neighbours or to poor wandering people (some of whom were sure to turn up at the wake). It was customary, too, that at least some of the clothes of the dead person were given away to the poor. It was fairly usual that a relative or friend of the dead wore a suit of his clothes to Mass on the three Sundays following the funeral, and there are places where a new suit was specially made for this purpose, with the belief and intention that the dead man would, thereby, be properly clothed in the next world.

One remarkable custom only recently laid aside in many parts of Ireland, and still to be heard in a few places, is the *Caoine*, the singing of a lament over the dead. Sometimes this was done only by the relatives, and according as each of these arrived he (or she) stood over the corpse and chanted lines expressing praise of the dead and sorrow at the death; the other relatives, or the general body of mourners, joined in a sort of chorus at certain places. Something like this–

'O father, you have left us! Ochón!
Why did you leave us? Ochón!
Or what did we do to you? Ochón!
That you went away from us? Ochón!

Tis you that had plenty! Ochón!
And why did you leave us? Ochón!
(all join in) Ochón! Ochón! Ullagón! Ó!!
Strong was your arm! Ochón!
Light was your step! Ochón!
Skilled were your hands! Ochón!
Poor we are without you! Ochon!
And why did you leave us? Ochon!
(all) Ochón, Ochón, Ullagón Ó!!'

In certain areas the *caoine* was sung not by the relatives but by old women of the place who were skilled in the art and who were encouraged during the performance of their office by an occasional glass of whiskey.

Perhaps the strangest feature of old-time wakes was the playing of wake games. These were party games like 'Hunt the Slipper' or 'Forfeits', and while some of them might be played at other times, many of them were played only at wakes. A typical one was 'The Bees and the Honey', in which an innocent 'gom' was chosen as the 'hive' and seated on a stool in the middle; he was then covered with straw and the 'bees' – other young men 'buzzed' around him searching for honey. Each 'bee' took a big mouthful of water and all together spilled their mouthfuls into the 'hive', thus soaking the poor wretch under the straw. Another was 'The Horse Fair' in which a number of boys and young men were 'horses' being put through their paces by a 'dealer', who called them appropriate names (a tall boy was the 'racehorse' and a stout youth the 'cob', a big rough fellow the 'shire' and an active young chap the 'colt') and made them show off tricks of running and jumping; if one failed he was beaten by the dealer, or made to lie on the floor while another player, the 'blacksmith', hammered the soles of his feet unmercifully. Other games were 'The Priest of the Parish', 'Buying the Oats', 'Fronsey Fronsey', 'Hot Hands', 'Fool in the Middle', 'Selling the Pig', 'The Poloney Man', and there were many more. Like so many other customs connected with death they must have come down from a very ancient time, perhaps, indeed, from the old Funeral Games of pre-Christian times. During the later 18th and all the 19th centuries the clergy spoke and acted against them as being 'pagan', 'disrespectful' and so on. But they were never meant to show anything other than respect for the dead in the ancient way, and like so many other old beliefs and practices they should be judged according to the standards of their time and not by those of our modern age.

The Funeral

The old people always said that you should never count
the number of mourners at a funeral, that if you did so
you would be 'counting them for your own funeral'.
But we felt that 'counting the cars' was not the same
thing, and that no risks were involved in it, and so we
always counted the cars. In those days, before there were
more than three or four motor-cars in the parish, any
vehicle was called a 'car'. Carts were 'common cars' and
the more elegant passenger conveyances were 'trap cars'
and 'side cars'. There were only a few side cars, and the
only 'back to back' in the district was the smart rig-out
in which the doctor made his rounds, but there were lots
of traps, and these, with common cars, figured in every
funeral. A small funeral had only five or six 'cars', but
there was a day when we counted as many as 117 in the
funeral of a man from one of the towns nearby who was
being buried with his people in our local churchyard.
Town and country were at that funeral. In those days
the motor-car was not popular at funerals. It raised dust.
It made too much noise. It could not regulate its pace
to that of the body of the funeral. If you had to have a
motor-car at a funeral (and most of us looked upon that
as showing off) you could go on ahead and wait at the
churchyard. What a change to our own day when many
an old person is carried to the grave at a speed greater
than any he ever reached while alive.

In those days the coffin was carried on men's shoulders. This was a mark of esteem; even when a hearse had been engaged – and we all agreed that the undertaker had as much right to make his living as the next man – it might be sent along in front for at least part of the distance. I have seen the hearse paid off and dismissed by the local men, and the coffin of a much respected old man carried seven miles to the graveyard on the shoulders of men who would not surrender that privilege for all the objections of the drivers of a couple of dozen motor-cars; that was in west Kerry, but the people of our parish showed their esteem in the same way. That is why a body of men walked directly behind the coffin in the traditional order of procession which was: first the coffin on men's shoulders, next a body of men walking, next women walking (if any of them wished to walk), then the vehicles, both traps and common cars, and last men mounted on horses. A large number of mounted men was a mark of especial prestige, but when many men went to funerals on bicycles and these were also relegated to the end of the procession, the pride of the mounted men fell off somewhat.

A hundred years ago the body was taken directly from the house to the graveyard, but gradually the custom came in of taking it to the church on the evening before the day of the burial. Thus there were two funerals, which had its own convenience for a community where attendance at the funeral was an important social duty. If you could be at both, well and good, if not you surely could put in an appearance at one or the other. The funeral from the house to the church was usually in the evening. Ours was a dairy-farming district, where all hands were needed at milking time, so the funeral to the church was late, to give time for people to wash and change. The funeral from the church to the graveyard and the burial were still regarded as the more important part, and this usually took place in the late forenoon or early afternoon, never in the early morning or late evening. If the body had to be brought from a distance – and some still come from the ends of the earth to lie with their own people – it spent the night in the local church and the funeral to the churchyard was at the usual time.

The grave had been dug that morning or the evening before. Two or three men of the neighbours volunteered to dig the grave, and some knowledgeable person went with them to point out the exact spot. This was very important, for no one wanted to be buried in the wrong place, and, besides, any encroachment on the graves of other families must be avoided. Digging the grave was a privilege, too, and you had to be careful to see that the right people did it, or you might offend good friends or neighbours. A grave was never dug after nightfall, or on a Monday unless one sod had been cut on the Sunday evening before. The sides of the grave were pared very smooth, the surface sods carefully set aside and the earth neatly banked up. A quantity of green grass was laid near at hand – this was to be spread on top of the coffin to deaden the sound of the clay falling upon it when the filling of the grave began. When all was ready the diggers laid spade and shovel crossed over the grave, with the ropes to lower the coffin into the grave coiled neatly on one side. Then they went home to change their clothes and be ready for the funeral, for it was their privileged task, too, to lower the coffin, fill the grave and replace the surface sods neatly upon it. Incidentally, one never said 'God bless the work' to men digging a grave, or indeed to any man working in a graveyard; the proper salutation was 'The Lord have mercy on the souls of the dead.'

Nowadays when the body is laid in the coffin the lid is put on inside the house. Formerly this was not so. The lid was taken off outside the door and placed leaning against the wall of the house. The coffin was taken inside and the body reverently lifted into it; a little pad of soft material was put under the head to raise it slightly. In this connection the tale was told of the mean-souled widow whose loud lamentations for appearance sake were interrupted by the sight of the servant boy rolling up a wisp of fine hay to make the head pad: 'Ulagón O! Ochón! &c. ... G'our that, you divil with the good hay and bring in a sop of the ould *fineán* from the end of the shtack!' You can imagine the outraged vehemence with which the people repeated the story.

The uncovered coffin was brought outside and laid on chairs in the farmyard while the relations and friends gathered round to take a last farewell and the keening women raised a last *ulagón*. Then the lid was screwed down and four near relatives raised the coffin and set off, while the rest of the procession formed up behind. Some neighbouring women stayed in the house to set all to rights, and as soon as the funeral had left the yard they bustled about opening windows, shaking out the bed-clothes where the corpse had lain, setting the clocks going again – for these had been stopped to show the exact time when the person had died, cleaning, sweeping and tidying away all signs of the wake. The chairs on which the coffin had rested were always overset as soon as the coffin was raised from them; these were now picked up and put in their usual places. A good fire was put down and a meal prepared for the return of the family and relatives.

As the funeral moved along the coffin bearers changed every hundred yards or so. There were many willing bearers, and they had already paired off so that men of the same stature went under it at the same time. There was a nicety to be observed here too; those who were nearest in friendship to the dead must take the first turns. The four nearest kin who carried the coffin from the house also took it into the church, and, next day, from the church and again into the graveyard. The coffin was carried at a fast marching pace – four to five miles an hour – and the changing of bearers was done without breaking the step, one pair changing at the time. When approaching the church a horseman rode ahead and began to toll the 'dead bell'.

Everybody wore his or her Sunday best at the funeral. A relative of the dead person handed out 'crapes' to selected mourners before the funeral; these were bands of black cloth which were then tied round the men's caps or hats. Priests who attended the funeral were given 'cypresses' – large pieces of white linen, about seven feet by four, folded and worn as sashes over the shoulder.

People meeting a funeral on the road should draw aside to let it pass. A cart or car should, if possible, be taken into a gateway or even into the field. People on foot drew aside until the head of the funeral had passed and then joined in to walk at least a few steps with it. Anybody who had to leave the procession should slip into a gateway or roadside gap until the whole funeral had passed by. The house doors were closed as the funeral approached, and those who had window blinds or curtains pulled them. In the village the shopkeepers had put up at least one shutter on each shop window, and the doors were closed.

There was a prescribed, traditional route from the church to the graveyard. The latter, as in so many Irish country places, was at the site of the old church destroyed in the persecutions of Elizabeth and Cromwell, and was still called the churchyard, although now a couple of miles from the village church. No short cuts were allowed, and no bad weather was permitted to interfere with the funeral; indeed rain was taken as a good omen. At the churchyard the coffin must not be taken directly from the gate to the graveside, but 'east to west by the south' along by the boundary wall, and then laid down on the north side of the grave while the priest read the service and led the prayers. Then it was lowered into the grave, the screws were unscrewed and laid on the lid, a good layer of green grass placed on top and the grave filled in and the sods replaced. Then spade and shovel were again laid in the form of a cross upon the grave mound and the people knelt to say a last prayer before dispersing. The near relatives and those who had come from a distance returned to the house and were hospitably entertained before they set out for home. Many of the people, before leaving the graveyard, went to the graves of their own dead to pray there.

In Memory of the Dead

Among the monuments of the past which are so frequent
a feature of the Irish scene some of the greatest were
erected as resting places and memorials for the dead.
There are the great mounds like Newgrange in County
Meath or Miscán Meabha on top of Knocknarea in
County Sligo, and the huge dolmens or cromlechs that
we know under names like 'the Long Woman's Grave'
or 'Dermot and Grainne's Bed'. All of these are sure
signs of the reverence and awe in which our distant fore-
fathers held their departed ones. We know, too, from
the smaller graves – the stone cists so often exposed by
the plough – that the humbler and less powerful people
took care to lay their dead away with concern and
respect, whether their motive was love for their dead
relatives or fear of what might happen if they did not
follow the proper ritual. We can follow the fashion
down through the ages, through the ogam stones with
their simple tale – 'The stone of Conan son of Lug' – and
the early Christian grave slaba with their equally brief
message 'A Prayer for Cuimín', through the carved and
decorated tombs of kings and bishops of the Middle
Ages down to the grave slabs and crosses of our grandfathers' time and our own. Whatever our ancestors'
faults may have been, disrespect for the dead was not
prominent among them.

Apart from the melancholy occasion of the funeral of
a friend or relative, we usually go into a graveyard either
to pray for the dead or to fulfil the equally pious duty of

clearing and tidying the family graves. It is sometimes said that we do not do either of these good works often enough. Be that as it may, it still is true that we very seldom visit a burying ground just to examine and admire the memorials there. And yet there may be many interesting things to see there. Often the whole history of a district or parish for hundreds of years may be seen there. There is the imposing tomb of the land-lord family that held sway for so long, but whose name is now seen only there. The tombstones of strong farmer families are here, with names added from one generation to the next to show how they weathered the bad times. There are stones of families once well-known, but now gone. There are simple crosses of wood or iron. There are headstones of priests still facing their congregation. There is the grave – if we know where to find it, for it is unmarked – of a poor wanderer who was found dead on the road in famine time. There are the graves of the soldier who fought for Britain in the Crimea and of the young man who died for his own country in the 'Troubles' and of the other young man whom we all knew who was killed under the blue flag of United Nations in Korea. We could sit down on a convenient slab and write the whole story of the last two or three hundred years from the stones and crosses around us.

Most of the inscriptions are simple enough. 'In memory of John Casey of Ballymore who died 8 April 1867 aged 86 years And of his wife Margaret who died 16 January 1883 aged 90 years And of their Son, Thomas Casey, died 22 June 1910'. Brief and to the point, but carrying a lot of family history. Of course we usually find 'I H S' at the top of the stone and 'R.I.P.'

at the bottom, and often a touching message like 'Erected by his sorrowing family' or 'Beloved by all his friends', but the whole story is a simple one, a worthy man or woman has died, and this is the memorial put up to mark the grave.

In former times, say a hundred and fifty years or so ago, inscriptions often were longer. Some of them carry a homily on death, a moralising verse such as –

> O Stranger pause when passing by
> As you are now so once was I
> As I am now so you shall be
> So be prepared to follow me.

Or this one in a County Kildare graveyard –

> Stay Passenger thy hastie foote
> This stone delivers thee
> A message from the famous twain
> That here intombed be
> Live well for vertue passeth welth
> As we doe find it now
> Riches beautie and worldlie state
> Must all to vertue bow.

There are many epitaphs in verse to be found. At Grey Abbey, County Down, a lady who died in 1707 is remembered by –

> Here Lies Jean Stay who night and day
> Was honest good and just.
> Her hope and love was from above
> In which place was her trust.
> Her spirit left her terrene part
> With joy to God where was her heart.

Not far away, at Donaghadee, is the grave of a sailor who

died in the same year, 1707, and under an anchor, the
sign of hope, are the lines: –

Tho Boreas blasts and Neptunes waves have tost me
to and fro
But now at length by God's decree I harbour here below.
Altho at anchor here I lie with many of our fleet
Yet once again I must set sail my Saviour Christ to meet.

And this sobering thought may be read on a stone at the
old churchyard of Drumcondra in Dublin –

> Nor tender youth nor heavy age
> Can shun the tyrant Death's dire rage
> Yet truth and sense this lesson give
> We live to die and die to live.

Most of us are well content to leave our memorials to
these who come after us, but it is clear that some
worthies of former days took no such chances. Witness
the stone at Kilconnell, County Galway, with the
message 'Pray for the soules of Lieftent Collonell Dear-
mott Daly of Killimur whoe erected this monument for
the use of himself and his brother Maijor Teige O Daly
and all there posterity 1674.' Or the stone in Kilfergus
graveyard in County Limerick, which we are told was
carved by the man himself with a verse of his own
composition –

> This is the grave of Tim Costello
> Who lived and died a right good fellow
> From his boyhood to his life's end
> He was the poor man's faithful friend
> He fawned before no purseproud clod
> He feared none but the living God
> And never did he do to others
> But what was right to do to brothers

He loved green Ireland's mountains bold
Her verdant vales and abbeys old
He loved her music song and story
He wept for her departed glory
And often did I hear him pray
That God would end her spoilers sway
To men like him may peace be given
In this world and in heaven   Amen

In north County Kerry, where in some graveyards
nearly every family has a tomb rather than a grave, one
sometimes sees an epitaph consisting of one word only,
the family name. Against that, some inscriptions are
very long indeed, like the one in St. Anne's Church in
Dublin, which bears forty-six lines extolling the virtues
and merits of two judges, Downes and Chamberlain. In
the same church is a monument to an exile from Saxony,
John Gotthelf Newman, who died in 1830 and is
commemorated on the stone by a poem of three verses
in German. In this matter of language it is curious to
note that hardly ever do we find a memorial inscription
in Irish. There are many in Latin and a few in French,
but although Irish was the spoken language of a large
proportion of the population two hundred years ago,
the inscriptions on the gravestones are almost invariably
in English, until our own century, when the Irish revival
gained force. Even Arthur O'Leary, on whom was
composed by his widow, Eibhlín Dubh Ní Chonaill a
very beautiful lament in Irish, has an English inscription
on his memorial at Kilcrea Abbey –

Lo, Arthur Leary, generous, handsome, brave,
Slain in his bloom, lies in this humble grave.

The shape and ornamentation of the stones and crosses

are often worth our interest. In the eighteenth century when the flamboyant, richly ornamented baroque style of art and architecture was all the fashion in the Catholic parts of Europe, some echoes of it reached our shores too, and many a humble stonecutter decorated his tombstones with scrolls and floral patterns, with cherubs and angels, with crucifixion and nativity scenes. Some of these are very beautiful, some naive, some even grotesque. Many have religious designs of various kinds, the I H S sign, the *Agnus Dei*, the Instruments of the Passion; this latter often includes the design of a cock rising from a pot, which is the representation of a well-known Irish legend – Our Lord's enemies mocked him after His death, saying 'He said He would rise again. He will as soon as that cock boiling in the pot rises!', whereon the cock jumped upon the rim of the pot and began to crow.

Sometimes we find handsome wooden crosses, but as wood does not last well in our climate, we can only guess at those that are gone, for most of the wooden ones we see are of recent date. Iron crosses last longer, and in the old days the blacksmiths regularly made grave crosses, some of them very shapely and well wrought. Then we have many stones which bear the symbol of the trade of the deceased. The smith himself may have, not an iron cross, but a stone with the hammer, tongs and anvil cut on it. We can find the shoemaker's last and knife and the shepherd's crook and shears and the farmer's plough. The chalice and patten usually figure on a priest's stone, and a schoolmaster may have an open book or even a figure from Euclid's geometry on his monument as a reminder of his learning.

There is one aspect of our care of the resting places of the dead which, in the recent past, strangers found it difficult to understand. We erected memorials without doubt, but often our attention to the graveyard ended there and many of them, especially the old graveyards at a distance from the churches in use at the time, were sorely neglected and overgrown with grass, weeds and briars, to the horror of many a returned exile making a pious pilgrimage to the graves of his forebears. Happily this is changing now, and one worthy object of both public and private enterprise is the proper care of the holy places where our dead are laid.

IRISH COUNTRY PEOPLE
Kevin Danaher

Irish Country People is simply one fascinating glorious feast of folklore and interesting sidelights of history recorded without a fraction of a false note or a grain of sentimentality. The topics covered in the twenty essays range over a wide field of history, folklore, mythology and archaeology. There are discussions about cures, curses and charms; lords, labourers and wakes; names, games and ghosts; prayers and fairy-tales. Nowadays we find it hard to visualise the dark winter evenings of those times when there was no electric light, radio, television or cinemas. We find it harder to realise that such evenings were not usually long enough for the games, singing, card-playing, music, dancing and story-telling that went on.

We can read about a six-mile traffic jam near Tailteann in the year 1168, just before the Norman invasion, and the incident is authenticated by a reference to the *Annals of the Four Masters*. The whole book is tinged with quiet humour: 'You should always talk to a dog in a friendly, mannerly way, but you should never ask him a question directly, for what would you do if he answered you, as well he might?'

FOLKTALES OF THE IRISH COUNTRYSIDE
Kevin Danaher

A delightful collection of tales simply told and suitable for the whole family.

THE YEAR IN IRELAND
IRISH CALENDAR CUSTOM
Kevin Danaher

This beautiful book describes how the round of the year with its cycle of festivals and seasonal work was observed in the Ireland of yesterday.

THE FARM BY LOUGH GUR
Mary Carbery

This book carries all the mists and memories, all the scent and sting of the Irish countryside.

THE BOOK OF IRISH CURSES
Patrick C. Power

The author has spent his life collecting the great curses of Ireland, and in this book he gives a history from earliest times to the present day.

A commentary and history is given with each curse.

GEMS OF IRISH WISDOM :
Irish Proverbs and Sayings
Padraic O'Farrell

Gems of Irish Wisdom is a fascinating collection of Irish proverbs and sayings.

The tallest flowers hide the strongest nettles.

The man who asks what good is money has already paid for his plot.

A man begins cutting his wisdom teeth the first time he bites off more than he can chew.

Even if you are on the right track, you'll be run over if you stay there.

The road to Heaven is well signposted but badly lit at night.

Love is like stirabout, it must be made fresh every day.

The begrudger is as important a part of Irish life as the muck he throws.

Love at first sight often happens in the twilight.

The man who hugs the altar-rails doesn't always hug his own wife.

If a man fools me once, shame on him. If he fools me twice shame on me.

God never closes one door but He opens another.

Hating a man doesn't hurt him half as much as ignoring him.

Every cock crows on his own dunghill.

A kind word never gets a man into trouble.